Books by Margaret Poynter

GOLD RUSH
The Yukon Stampede of 1898

SEARCH & RESCUE
The Team and the Missions

TOO FEW HAPPY ENDINGS
The Dilemma of the Humane Societies

VOYAGER
The Story of a Space Mission

(with Arthur L. Lane)
(with Arthur L. Lane)

TOO FEW
HAPPY
ENDINGS

TOO FEW HAPPY ENDINGS

The Dilemma of the Humane Societies

by MARGARET POYNTER

Atheneum 1981 New York

*Photographs courtesy of
Pasadena Humane Society.*

LIBRARY OF CONGRESS CATALOGING IN PUBLICATION DATA

Poynter, Margaret.
Too few happing endings:
the dilemma of the humane societies.

SUMMARY: Discusses the critical problem of pet
overpopulation and stray animals; the humane
societies, animal shelters, and individuals that
deal with it; and its effect on each of us.
1. Animals, Treatment of—Societies, etc.—
Juvenile literature. [1. Animals—Treatment—
Societies, etc.] I. Title.
HV4702.P69   636.08′3   81-2239
ISBN 0-689-30864-7   AACR2

To MARK,
*for finding that stray puppy
and bringing her home.*

Contents

1 · Protector or Destroyer?   *3*

2 · How It All Began   *9*

3 · A Matter of Justice   *17*

4 · "You Are the Force in
    This City"   *23*

5 · "Overworked, Underpaid
    Dynamite People"   *40*

6 · Animal Problems, People
    Problems   *49*

7 · "It's Raining Cats and Dogs!"   *59*

8 · Cat People and Dog People   *70*

9 · "There's a Noise in My
    Chimney!"   *86*

vii

10 · Some Happy Endings *94*

11 · A Beloved Pet or a Disposable
      Object? *105*

12 · "Where, Oh Where Can
      He Be?" *116*

13 · More Than a Million
      Dog Bites *122*

      INDEX

TOO FEW
HAPPY
ENDINGS

1

Protector
or Destroyer?

IT'S JUST two minutes after eight in the morning,
and the telephone is already ringing in the office
of the county animal shelter. As the clerk takes
the call, Steve, an animal control officer, is preparing
to leave on his rounds. The office door opens, and a
young man enters the room and approaches the coun-
ter. There's a mixed breed shepherd at his side.

"Can I help you?" Steve asks.

"My landlord told me I have to get rid of my
dog," the man replies. "I can't find a place where pets
are allowed, and none of my friends want to be
bothered with a dog this big. I don't want to leave her
here, but what else can I do?"

Steve hands him a release form. "We'll try to
find her a good home, but I have to tell you that we

might have to put her to sleep."

The man nods. "I know, I know. But the only other choice I have is to dump her on a street corner somewhere."

"You're doing the right thing," Steve says. "I've seen how an abandoned animal has to live, and you wouldn't want that to happen to your dog."

The man signs his name to the release form, then kneels beside the dog and puts his arm around her neck. The dog licks his cheek and her tail thumps on the wooden floor. Two minutes later a kennel worker clips a leash onto her collar and leads her to the back door. The young man rises and leaves the office, but not before Steve sees the glint of tears in his eyes.

The dog tries to follow him, but is stopped by a tug on the leash. She looks bewildered, but obediently follows the kennel worker. Steve turns away. He wonders if he'll ever become hardened to such scenes.

The door opens again. A middle-aged, poorly dressed woman comes in carrying a box. "That cat of mine had another batch of kittens," she says, "and I couldn't find homes for any of them."

"Are you going to have the mother spayed?" the clerk asks.

"I can't afford it," the woman replies.

The clerk hands her a booklet. "Please read this. It tells you all about our low-cost spay and neuter clinics."

The woman signs the release form. "I'll think about it," she says.

Steve notices that she doesn't take the booklet with her when she leaves the office. He knows that she'll probably be back with another batch of kittens before the end of the year. At least, she brings them to us, he thinks. That's better than leaving them behind a grocery store or in a park.

Meanwhile, another clerk has been busy answering the telephone. "There's a dead dog in my front yard," a woman caller says.

A man calls. "There's a big dog chained up in the yard down the street. The owner's been gone for almost a week. I've been throwing food over the fence, but I'm afraid to get too close to him."

Another call is from the owner of a stable. Someone drove a car through the fence of his corral, and two horses are loose on the streets of the suburbs.

When Steve is ready to leave, the clerk hands him the list of messages. Steve wonders how he's going to find time to also round up the strays that plague the west end of town.

He walks through the back door of the office and past the rows of cages that house the scores of dogs and cats. A springer spaniel pokes his nose through the chain link wiring of his enclosure. A scraggly little white poodle yaps for attention. A Labrador huddles in the corner of her cage, but she gazes after

Steve as he passes by. She has learned to accept the fact that most people are too busy to stop and pet her.

Steve looks in on an old pit bull terrier that he picked up two days ago. Its sturdy body is scarred from dozens of dog fights. "Too bad, old boy," Steve murmurs. "You'd have made someone a great pet." He tries to block out the memory of another pit bull. By the time Steve found him, he was already dead, his throat torn open by his opponent's slashing teeth.

What kinds of person turns dogs into killers of other dogs? Steve wonders.

He doesn't linger in front of any of the other cages, because he's afraid he'll become too fond of the dogs and cats inside of them. And if he does, how will he bear the thought of them being put down?

Put down. Put to sleep. Euthanise. Steve shakes his head as he thinks of those soft sounding words. He knows that the correct word is "kill," but he finds it hard to use such a harsh term. He realizes that the killing is necessary, especially for the old, sick, and badly injured animals. And even for the young and healthy ones, a quick, merciful death is certainly better than being half alive in a bad home or on the streets.

Still, the killing bothers Steve. When he took this job, he thought he was going to be a protector of animal life. He soon found that he is part of a system that destroys many more animals than it saves. And whenever Steve thinks about that, rage wells up inside him. His anger is directed both at himself and at the careless pet owners who create the necessity for such a system.

Steve looks at his watch. It's getting late and he has a lot to do. Then he hears voices, that of a woman and a small boy who are walking up and down the aisles between the cages.

"Now remember," the woman says, "pick out a small dog. Our fence isn't high enough to keep a big one in the yard. We don't want our pet to get into the street, do we?"

Steve watches them as the boy studies each dog intently. The air is filled with plaintive whines and frantic barks. "Pick me! Pick me!" all the animals seem to be crying.

The mother and son stop in front of a cage that contains a black cocker mix. The boy grins. "That's the one," he says. "That's the one I want!" He puts his fingers through an opening in the enclosure and the dog licks them.

"Are you certain?" the mother asks. "A dog isn't like a football or a skateboard, you know. You can't throw it away or trade it off if you get tired of it."

"I'm sure," the boy says. "This is the one."

Steve smiles as he walks toward his truck. Just a little over a week ago he had found that little cocker caught in some barbed wire along the side of a busy highway. If it had remained in the shelter just a few more days, it would have been put down. Now it was going to live out its life in a good home.

Steve suddenly feels a little better about his job. He walks briskly toward his truck, prepared to handle whatever the day brings.

2

How It All Began

URING THE COURSE of a shift, an animal control officer has to attend to many jobs. One of the most important ones is ridding the streets of stray dogs. Actually, by the time an officer checks up on reported dog bite cases, takes care of animal emergencies, and investigates complaints about leash law violations, he usually spends only a small part of his day hunting strays. The chances are poor that any particular homeless dog will ever end up in an animal control truck. There are just too many strays and too few people whose job it is to round them up.

A look at the statistics gives an indication of how big the problem is. One survey indicated that there are at least 25 million stray dogs and cats in the United States today. A town that contains fifty thousand human residents probably has 100 to 300 stray dogs at any one time, and about half of the owned animals are allowed to run loose also.

Sprawling Los Angeles County in California has six tax-supported animal shelters and thousands of strays, but only forty-seven officers to cover both day and night shifts. In New York City, it's estimated that there are one hundred fifty thousand stray dogs. To handle this situation, there are only eight people to capture them. These humane technicians or "drivers," as they call themselves, are experts in the art of dog catching. They have to be, because many of the animals have had to become feral, or half wild, in order to survive. There's an irony here, because it was survival that caused dogs and cats to become domesticated in the first place. Their relationship with humans came about because man and animal needed each other's help in coping with a largely hostile world.

Prehistoric people lived in constant fear of marauding animals. They were afraid to sleep, because not to hear a stealthy footfall could mean death. There was, however, a wolflike creature that appeared to be harmless. Packs of these shaggy-haired, sharp-eyed animals had formed the habit of encircling the tribal camp during meal times. They waited patiently while the humans gnawed at the bones they had torn from the carcass of their captured prey. When the meal was over, the men tossed the remnants in the direction of the animals. Soon the sounds of snarling and snapping filled the air, but the members of the tribe weren't afraid. They had never seen one of the savage-looking beasts attack even a defenseless child. Far from being a danger, the creatures created a barrier between the humans and the man-eating animals that prowled the plains.

As time passed, the wolflike creatures lost their fear of man. They inched closer and closer to the campfire. One day, their leader took food directly from the hand of a tribal member. The sun had risen and set only a few more times before a human child and a wolf pup were seen gamboling together in a clearing. Later, that pup must have found its way into a cave that sheltered the child's family. The move was inevitable, because, by then, man was used to the protection that the animal provided, and the animals had grown dependent upon the food that man gave to them.

Eventually, the wolflike creatures did more than just protect the humans. They learned to guard supplies, haul burdens, and track down prey. Some of them were smarter than others, or were physically better able to perform certain tasks. The humans took special care of these more valuable animals and encouraged them to breed. Thus, the many types of modern dogs began to evolve. Hounds are still used for hunting and tracking, shepherds for herding cattle, and huskies for hauling heavy sleds.

When the Phoenicians took to the sea, their dogs went with them. Many of the animals were left in foreign ports, where they increased in number. The Romans took their well-trained four-footed soldiers with them when they went on campaigns to conquer barbarian territories. Dogs were used to guard supplies along the rear lines. Wearing specially made armor, they led attacks in the front lines.

More than any other creature, the dog proved to be adaptable to the needs of man. It was also able to adapt to various climates and topographies. The dogs that were raised in the Arctic protected themselves by growing thick, two-layer coats. In the warm and humid tropics, they grew thin, sparse coats, and in a few cases, had no hair at all. The runners and hunters developed long legs and slim, streamlined bodies. The rodent-catching terriers developed short legs. Dogs that were used as draft animals had broad, heavily muscled shoulders. The ones that were used for tracking developed an extra keen sense of smell.

The dog was not only adaptable in its physical make-up but it also seemed to have no trouble in transferring its allegiance from its own pack leader to its human masters. As a result, men found the dog to be an extremely loyal servant, and the partnership they formed was a strong one. One historian went so far as to say, "It would appear that man was able to fight his way up from a state of nature to civilization only with the aid of the dog."

Is that statement an exaggeration? The early settlers of the Arctic probably wouldn't think so. Without dogs, it's possible the opening of this harsh and isolated territory might have had to wait hundreds of years.

The dog was domesticated at least fifteen thousand years ago. Man's close relationship with the cat began about ten thousand years later. It too was born out of a mutual need. The cat needed man's protection. Man needed the cat to keep rodents out of his home and his stores of grain. The ancient Egyptians of the Nile Valley valued cats so much that they worshipped them as gods.

Cats traveled along with dogs on the ships of the Phoenicians, and the rodent-hating Romans took them to Britain when they invaded that island. To their surprise, they found that cats were already firmly established there.

Many people worshipped and valued cats, but there were also many people who hated them. They thought they were evil creatures, sneaky and untrustworthy. As the Middle Ages approached, more and more people believed that cats represented paganism, witchcraft, sorcery and black magic. It was said that some cats were witches in disguise, and they were blamed for everything from crop failures to destructive acts of nature. During this period, thousands of cats were hunted down and either drowned or burned at the stake. The audience cheered while the tormented creatures writhed and yowled. The more they suffered, the better luck their torturers were supposed to have.

The slaughtered cats had their revenge during the fifteenth century. So many of them had been destroyed that the rat population was able to multiply by hundreds and thousands. It was these hordes of rats that helped to spread the Black Plague, which killed much of the human population of Europe.

During the following two centuries the hatred of cats subsided, and people were glad to welcome them into their homes and fields. Many famous artists and writers praised the feline grace, charm, agility and beauty.

Despite the early partnership between men and cats and dogs, most people still looked upon them as they did upon all animals. They were considered only as objects or possessions and were thought to have no more feeling than a table or a wagon. Although many working animals were well cared for, almost as many were beaten, and half starved. Unless its owner was prosperous, an old dog or horse that had become use-less was often abandoned.

The Industrial Revolution made the plight of animals even worse. At that time, thousands of people left their farms and went to the cities to work in factories. Many of them brought their favorite cats and dogs with them, then found that feeding them was too great an expense. During the day, the animals searched for scraps in the gutters. Dog waste accumulated and children were bitten. Puppies and kittens soon added to the problem, and strays became common sights.

The selectmen of Boston despaired about the "curst and unruly doggs and bitches. . . ." They passed laws that were supposed to control the problem, but no one paid any attention to them. In another New England town the mayor made a desperate effort to "get some Persons to bury all the dead dogs . . . that lye in the streets." Not many people applied for the job.

During the nineteenth century the problem got out of hand in some of the larger cities. Every summer there were so many dog bite victims that the officials of New York City declared war on all dogs, sick or well. Any dog that ran when it was chased, or that opened its mouth to pant was presumed to be rabid. The official dog catchers were joined by private citizens, who received fifty cents for each dog they killed, whether that dog was dangerous or not.

This early method of animal control was very effective, but even then there were many people who were sickened at the brutal way in which it was performed. One of them was to go down in history as the founder of the humane movement in the United States.

3

A Matter of Justice

THIS COUNTRY's humane movement was started because of the suffering of horses, not the suffering of cats and dogs. It was initiated by Henry Bergh, a man who didn't particularly care about any sort of animal, but who did care a great deal about justice. And it gained much of its momentum, not necessarily because of the misery of dumb creatures, but because of a widespread reaction to human misery.

For the first half of his life, Henry Bergh had showed no sign of becoming involved in humane work, or in any other kind of work. Since he had inherited plenty of money, he could afford to spend his days going to the theater, visiting art galleries and museums, and drinking tea with his many friends. Both before and after the Civil War, he often traveled to Europe. On some of these trips, he acted as a representative of the United States government. He enjoyed meeting important people in the various embassies and attending the lavish parties and dances.

He also liked to travel along the roads of France and Russia and watch the peasants bow as he passed them in his official carriage. One day he saw one of the peasants beating an old, bony horse. He called to his driver to stop, then got out and spoke to the man.

"This horse has no doubt served you well," he said. "Is this the way to repay her faithful service?"

The peasant apologized, astounded that such an important-looking man would be concerned about a worthless mare. Bergh himself would have been astounded if he had known that the encounter was destined to change the course of his life. His sense of justice had been aroused, and his eyes had been fully opened to the instances of cruelty to animals that were so common all over Europe.

When Bergh returned to the United States, he realized that animal abuse was just as common in his own country. In New York City, for instance, the horses that pulled the streetcars were usually half-starved, overworked and lame. They received relief only when they finally collapsed in their tracks and died.

Bergh found many other kinds of cruelties. He saw cattle and pigs crowded into small pens near the stockyards. Although the temperature often rose to over one hundred degrees, there was no water for the animals to drink. He saw cats and dogs being drowned, kicked, stoned, and burned alive, with no one raising a voice against their tormentors. He saw living sea tortoises tied in place by means of ropes threaded through holes drilled in their fins.

When Bergh found that there was no law against any of these cruelties, he went into action. There were no more long evenings at the theater, no more parties, and no leisurely journeys. All of his time was used in the work that was to consume the rest of his life.

His first goal was to convince the New York State legislators of the necessity for an animal protection law. To accomplish it, he went to everyone he knew and asked for their money and support. Soon strangers were offering to help him in his campaign. Many of these were men and women who had been sickened by all of the human suffering and death that had occurred during the Civil War. They were looking forward to a more peaceful and humane era, in which all living creatures would be treated fairly.

Bergh quickly reached his first goal. In 1866, the New York Legislature passed this country's first animal protection law. At the same time, it approved the charter for Bergh's American Society for the Prevention of Cruelty to Animals (ASPCA), the first humane organization in the western hemisphere. Bergh knew that his real work had just begun. Besides becoming the society's president, he became its hardest working fund-raiser, organizer, promoter, and enforcer of the new humane law.

Although he had to spend much time in his office, Bergh was most enthusiastic when he was patrolling the streets, armed with a copy of the new ordinance. Early in the morning and late in the evening, he could be seen searching for animal abusers. When he saw a wagon driver beating a horse, Bergh threaded his way across the busy boulevard to speak to him. "My friend," he began, "you can't do that anymore."

The driver was usually much taller and stronger than the slim, frail-looking Bergh. "Can't beat my own horse?" he might shout. "The devil I can't!"

Bergh seldom raised his voice. "You're probably not aware that you're breaking the law, but you are. I could have you arrested. I only want to inform you what a risk you run."

Unlike the apologetic European peasant, an American wagon driver was likely to respond to Bergh with a raised whip or a clenched fist. No threat was enough to make Bergh back down, however. The confrontations usually ended without violence, with the horse beater muttering, "You're mad," as he left the scene.

Bergh became used to being called a madman. He also learned to ignore the derisive laughter that was aimed at him. One newspaper columnist predicted that Bergh would soon be asking people to willingly share their meals and their homes with goats, rats, and cockroaches.

Such articles often backfired on the author and gave the humane movement added publicity and support. Following Bergh's example, other people formed societies and by 1877 there were twenty-seven of them, widely scattered from New Hampshire to California. In that year, the American Humane Association (AHA) was formed. Its purpose was, and still is, to serve as a clearinghouse for all of the local humane agencies. It also worked on especially difficult cases, such as bringing about laws to enforce humane methods of transporting livestock from one state to another.

HENRY BERGH got this country's humane movement off to a running start. If he were here today, what would he think about the progress of that movement? Of course, he'd be pleased to see that the ASPCA is still functioning in New York City; that there are thousands of dedicated people who work in the field of animal protection; that every state now has laws against cruelty to animals; and that there are many local and several national humane organizations that were formed to enforce those laws.

Bergh would certainly visit some of the thousands of animal shelters that house this country's lost and unwanted cats and dogs as well as other domestic creatures and often a variety of wildlife. He would nod his head in approval at the way most of these shelters care for these animals. He would no doubt be shocked to find that there are others staffed by lazy, negligent, and ignorant people. The animals in these shelters are suffering, Bergh would think. Why is this situation allowed to continue? Why don't the people in this community do something about it?

Certainly Bergh wouldn't hesitate to do something about it. Pulling out a copy of the humane laws, he'd corner the manager of the shelter, point to an injured, half-starved dog in a filthy cage, and say, "My friend, you can't do that anymore!"

And there are people today who are doing just that.

4

"You Are the Force in This City"

THE HUMANE SOCIETY inspector was over two blocks away from the animal shelter, but she could already smell a dreadful odor. She remembered what the complaint had said. "I had to hold my breath when I walked into that place. Don't they ever clean out the cages?"

When the inspector entered the office, she saw that the shelter manager and three employees were engrossed in a game of cards.

"What can I do for you, lady?" the manager asked.

"Mind if I look around?" said the inspector.

The manager shrugged. "Sure, go ahead. If you see something you like, let us know. There's a lot of good dogs and cats back there, and they all need homes." He turned his attention back to his cards.

The inspector left the office. Her stomach was churning, both from the smell of uncollected animal waste and from anger. She walked up and down the aisles and grew still angrier, because she could see that almost every rule of humane animal care was being broken. Two full-grown German shepherds were sharing a cramped cage with three much smaller dogs. A short-haired terrier was shivering in a corner, his bones sharply outlined against his skin. Was he sick? Or had he been bullied by the larger dogs into giving up his share of the food?

A dachshund in the next cage had a torn ear that was beginning to show signs of infection. The floor of every enclosure was dotted with piles of dried and fresh feces, and the walls were splattered with the filth. One small enclosure contained eight dogs, and the inspector noticed that one of them had yellow, runny matter seeping from its eyes and nose. Distemper, she thought. Why in the world hasn't he been isolated from the others?

As she approached the last row of cages, a dog fight broke out. The snarls and cries of pain brought two shelter workers out of the office. One of them turned on a hose and separated the two animals by playing a strong stream of water on them. There was no attempt to dry them off afterward. The drenched dogs huddled in opposite corners of their cage and shivered violently, while the two workers returned to their card game.

The inspector had seen more than enough. She followed the men into the office and confronted the manager. "Are you aware that there have been complaints about the treatment of the animals in this shelter?" she asked. "I'm from the humane society, and from what I've seen in the last few minutes, the complaints are well founded."

The manager stared at her. "What do you mean? I'm paid to get these mutts off the street and lock them up, and that's exactly what I do."

"You're supposed to do more than just keep them locked up," replied the inspector. "You're supposed to see that they get humane care. Those cages are much too crowded, you have a sick animal back there that should be put into a cage by himself, and at least two of those dogs are half starved."

"They were that way when they came in," the manager said.

"Maybe they were, but they're going to stay that way unless you separate them from the larger animals." The inspector paused for a moment. "Look, I'm going to make you an offer. We'll send a crew of people out here to help you get this place cleaned up. They'll show you and your staff how a shelter should be run."

The manager rubbed his chin. "And what if I don't take you up on your offer?"

"Then we'll take legal action to force you to do it. We don't want to go that far, but we will if it's necessary."

"Well. . . ." The manager was silent for a moment. "Guess I don't have much of a choice, do I? When will your crew get here?"

THERE ARE SOME EXCELLENT animal shelters in our country. The ones that are accredited by the Humane Society of the United States (HSUS) not only take the best possible care of the animals they handle, but also do an excellent job of educating people about responsible pet ownership.

There are many shelters that provide the same high quality of animal care but fail to teach the public about the importance of spaying and neutering, and of keeping their pets at home.

There are also shelters that seem to excel only in animal neglect and cruelty. Phyllis Wright, who is the animal control director of the HSUS, says of this type of shelter, "I've seen more cruelties inside some so-called animal havens than I have in many other places in which animals are kept. We're dealing with living, feeling creatures that are in jail through no fault of their own. They don't deserve to be subjected to disease, dogfights, freezing cold, and near starvation."

"You are the force in this city," Mrs. Wright once told a group of citizens. "We can come from the outside and reinforce you, but you are the taxpayers who really own the shelter. Only you have the power to change the way it's run."

What kind of animal shelter does your community have? Are the animals treated humanely? Or are they suffering? You don't have to be an expert in the humane sciences to be able to judge whether or not the people who work there are doing their jobs well.

Visit your local shelter. As you approach it, take a deep breath. The first clue to a badly run facility is the terrible smell that results from uncollected animal waste and sickness. A good shelter may smell of disinfectant, but otherwise it will be almost odorless.

Use your eyes as well as your nose. Are the animals separated according to size? If large and small dogs are mixed together, you can be sure that the smaller ones aren't getting enough to eat.

Do the animals have enough room to sit and lie down comfortably? Are they able to get enough exercise? Are the sick animals separated from the healthy ones?

The cats should have litter boxes, because they

have a compulsion to bury their waste. Without litter or dirt, cats have been known to tear out their claws as they attempt to dig holes in the cement floors of their cages. Cats should also be given cat food, not big chunks of dry dog food, which they may not be able to chew or swallow.

Are the cages clean? When they are hosed down, are the animals first removed? Shivering, wet dogs are miserable, and they could easily become ill.

Do the people at your shelter act as if they like their jobs and take pride in what they're doing? Or do they spend most of their time in the front office visiting with each other?

When you're finished with your inspection, ask yourself one more question. "If *my* pet had to spend some time here, how would I feel about the way he was treated?" The answer to that query will be your final judgment about whether the shelter is good, bad, or in between.

If you don't like what you've seen, talk to your parents and ask them to take a look at the shelter. If you belong to a youth group such as the Scouts, the "Y", or a school organization, talk to the other members and to your leader or counselor. The more people you can get interested in your campaign, the more chance there will be of getting some changes made.

Make a detailed list of all of the inhumane acts and conditions in the shelter, and have everyone else do the same. Next, show these lists to the shelter manager. It often helps to have an adult with you at this time.

If the manager doesn't seem cooperative, send the list of complaints to the Humane Society of the United States, at 2100 L Street, N.W., Washington, DC, 20037. And remember, the complaints must be written down in detail. It isn't enough to say, "The animals are suffering." You must give times, dates, and descriptions, such as were given in the following HSUS inspectors' reports.

"On December 13, at 4 P.M., I found three containers of wet, moldy food, which contained numerous maggots. Four employees were at the shelter, but only one appeared to be doing any work. The others stood near the front gate or in the office talking to the clerk."

"Cages used to house cats were so small that a confined mother cat could not stand, sit, or lie down in a natural position."

"There were thirty-seven dogs in a pen measuring ten feet by ten feet. The animals ranged in size from fifteen to eighty pounds. Numerous dog fights took place with various degrees of injury. The injuries were not treated for several hours. Observed

March 3, 9:30 A.M."

"One pound of food was put in a cage with twenty-three dogs, causing horrendous dog fights. In three and a half minutes there wasn't one scrap of food left. There had been five fights. One Great Dane had taken five dogs and just slammed them up against a wall and stood over the feeding trough."

"We observed a filthy, fly-infested cesspool on our November 10 inspection. We observed feces not removed, making the animals live in their own waste."

Several well-written and documented letters of complaint are enough to trigger an HSUS investigation. One of its inspectors will visit the facility and file an official report on its current condition. If the animals are still being neglected, a crew will be sent to show the staff how to bring the shelter up to humane standards. The members of the crew will give practical demonstrations on the proper way to clean a cage and to feed a group of animals. They will show films and give classes on the basic needs of animals. They will instruct the manager about such facts as how many square feet should be allowed for each dog and cat.

When the HSUS crew has finished its job at one shelter, its members will move on to their next assignment. After a few weeks, other inspectors will visit each shelter to make certain that its staff hasn't returned to its old bad habits.

Just following up on complaints about poorly run shelters is a big job, but the HSUS does much more than that. Its employees look into *any* reported case of animal abuse. They have been responsible for improvements in the treatment of animals that are used in rodeos and in the movies. They are fighting a long uphill battle against the cruel "sports" of dog racing, cock fighting, and dog fighting. They are trying to eliminate "factory farming" in which animals must live out their lives in cages so small that they can't turn around or lie down. They have done much toward letting people know about the misuse of drugs in horse races. There are still many horses that are injured, but are given pain killing injections to keep them running.

HSUS employees visit municipal zoos and give suggestions on how to improve the animals' environment. When a lion is displayed in a large grotto that has caves and shrubs, or an antelope is given a hill to climb, they are much more content. Such surroundings also give the public a better idea of the natural habitat of a wild animal.

The HSUS often has long struggles with the owners of "roadside zoos," or privately owned collections of wild animals. There are at least one thousand of these "menageries of misery" scattered throughout the United States in tourist areas. A roadside zoo is different from a government-owned zoo in that the animals are exhibited, not for educational purposes, but only to make money for someone. They are usually used as a "come-on" to entice people into the owner's main business, which is often a restaurant, a gift shop, or a carnival.

The owners of such zoos rarely know how to care for a wild animal. They don't know what its diet should be, or how to recognize signs of illness, and they often don't care. If the business fails, some of them have simply walked away and left the animals to starve to death. One HSUS investigator found several animals that had been left in the middle of a midwestern winter without food, water, or heat.

Joe, an American black bear, had to live for six months in a cage so small that he couldn't stand up. The bottom of his cage was covered with his own waste and he had developed ulcers on his feet. His owner's idea of a proper bear diet was candy bars, doughnuts, and soda pop. When an HSUS investigator rescued Joe, the lock on his cage had to be sawed off because it had rusted shut.

Today this bear is living a good life in an animal orphanage, but there are many more creatures who still are just existing under his former miserable living conditions.

The work of the HSUS won't be done until there are no more animals suffering at the hands of man. That day will come sooner if more people become aware of their responsibility toward, not only dogs and cats, but toward every creature, either wild or domesticated. The HSUS needs all of our eyes and ears and awareness and caring if it is going to be able to accomplish its goals.

Phyllis Wright is the Director of Animal Sheltering and Control for the HSUS. HSUS PHOTO

The shelter workers will feed and house this dog, but what he really needs is a good permanent home.

Feeding time at an animal shelter gives the animals one of their few human contacts.

The kennel worker's touch is gentle, but this dog knows that there is something wrong.

About half the "owned" dogs that are picked up by animal control officers are never claimed by their owners. TERRY ANDRUES

It's difficult for an animal shelter worker not be become fond of the puppies that are waiting for adoption.

TERRY ANDRUES

*This puppy is part of
a litter that never should
have been born.*

Many of the animals brought into animal shelters have been neglected by their owners. This dog was suffering from malnutrition.

There won't be any more dog fights for this old bull terrier. A pit bull rescue association will try to find him a good home. TERRY ANDRUES

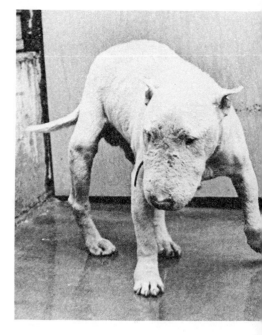

This puppy had been stolen by a man who wanted to train it for dog fighting. Animal control officers rescued it, and its owner has been notified. TERRY ANDRUES

Dogs and cats aren't the only creatures that end up in an animal shelter.

5

"Overworked, Underpaid Dynamite People"

ONE AFTERNOON several years ago, a distraught woman rushed into the office of a Humane Society animal shelter in Northern California. She was cradling a shoe box in her arms. Nestled on a piece of old blanket inside the box was a nine-week-old, black-and-white kitten.

"Can you help him?" the woman asked the clerk. "Some boys in my neighborhood were taking turns throwing the poor thing against a wall." She shuddered. "They killed two others before I had a chance to stop them."

The clerk stroked the battered kitten's head with her forefinger. She was surprised to hear a loud purr. "He's a spunky one," she said. "A real dynamo. I have a hunch he's going to be all right."

The news about the injured kitten spread throughout the shelter, and all of the employees thought that Dynamo was the perfect name for such a brave little creature. As the shelter's veterinarian was examining him, Dynamo had eighteen people rooting for him.

The diagnosis turned out to be a mixture of both good and bad news. "He's in pretty good shape," the veterinarian announced. "There are no internal injuries, but he does have a broken leg. The problem is, of course, that we don't have an x-ray, or the anesthetic, or the steel pins that are necessary to repair the break."

Everyone knew that the shelter also didn't have enough money to pay for a private vet to perform the surgery. Was the kitten going to have to be destroyed after all? Its fate was decided when the veterinarian reached into his pocket and pulled out $25. "I'll chip in this much toward the cost of the operation," he said.

That was all the encouragement that the other employees needed. They dug into their pockets and handbags, and the money was quickly raised. The surgery was scheduled for the following morning, and for the rest of the afternoon and far into the evening, Dynamo was seldom alone. The shelter workers gave up their breaks and stayed beyond the end of their shifts so they could watch over him. The kitten seemed to forget his pain as he responded to their strokes and nibbled at the tender pieces of meat that they offered to him.

"He's eating up a storm," a kennel worker reported in delight.

The next day that delight turned into despair, because Dynamo died on the operating table. The anesthetic had caused his tiny lungs to become starved for oxygen, and his small size prevented the vet from inserting an air hose into his chest. All of Dynamo's benefactors grieved for him, but they didn't regret the time or the money they had spent in the effort to save his life. The important thing is that they had made the attempt and that the kitten had been surrounded by love during the last few hours of his short life. Perhaps that love had partially made up for the pain that his tormentors had caused him to endure.

"OVERWORKED, underpaid, dynamite people." That's the way the supervisor of this shelter describes the people who work there. This deep concern for one injured kitten is typical of the concern they have for all of the animals in their care. Kennel workers cut short their lunch breaks so they can check on the cleanliness of the cages. The people in the education department visit schools to teach young people the proper care of animals. The staff of the spay and neuter clinic conducts an ongoing war against dog and cat overpopulation. Every possible effort is made to find the owners of the licensed dogs that are brought into the shelter. The woman whose job it is to locate those owners often works at home after she has finished her regular eight hour shift. She has found that it's easier to find people at home during the evening.

Sometimes she's successful at finding the owner, but that success turns into failure when no one turns up to retrieve the animal. Evidently that owner doesn't want to pay the impoundment fines, or perhaps he's happy to be rid of a troublesome pet. It's too easy to get another one when the time is more convenient.

About half the dogs that the animal control officers bring into this shelter are owned dogs, but many of them wait in vain for their owners to take them home.

This shelter's adoption expert also works overtime screening potential pet owners. She thoroughly examines the answers they write on the questionnaire she gives them.

Do you have a fenced yard? (If the answer is no, the prospective owner will probably be turned down.)

Do you live in a house, or an apartment? (An

apartment dweller should forget about adopting an Irish setter. A poodle would be more suitable.)

Is there a small child in the family? (A toddler shouldn't be given a helpless puppy or kitten.)

Are you able to afford the food bills and medical expenses that go along with pet ownership?

Have you ever owned a pet before? If so, what happened to it? (The adoption expert can tell a lot about an applicant by looking at the answer to this question.)

Why do you want a pet? (Too many people say, "To teach my child responsibility." And too often, that child learns only irresponsibility. An animal is much more than a teaching tool.)

The shelter supervisor himself often works a twelve or sixteen hour day, because he won't go home until every emergency has been taken care of, and until he feels that every animal has been given the best possible care. If all shelters were staffed with the kind of people who work here, the job of the HSUS would be much easier.

The excellence of this shelter is equalled by many other shelters in various parts of the United States. Their excellence doesn't keep some people from being critical of them, however. Some of the criticism is helpful, and the manager of a good shelter will use it to make his shelter even better. But some of it is a result of the critic's lack of understanding of the problems that the people who work with stray animals must face day after day.

One of these problems is a constant one—that of a lack of money. Animal control and care usually come far down on the list of things that city and county officials feel are important. Thus, while the number of stray cats and dogs keeps growing larger, the funds to care for them keep getting smaller. Somehow, the people involved in animal control must stretch those funds enough to try to keep the streets clear of dangerous strays; to rescue wild animals from fire and flood and oil spills; to aid horses and other farm animals when they get into trouble; to investigate dog bite incidents; to sponsor spaying and neutering clinics; to settle pet-related arguments between neighbors; to follow up on reports about cruelty to animals; to handle the sale of licenses; and to give out citations to pet owners who violate the leash laws.

To make the situation more difficult, animal control officers and shelter employees are often caught in the middle of a continuing battle between people who love cats and dogs and who believe their pets should be welcomed anywhere they themselves are, and the animal haters who think that cats and dogs shouldn't be allowed to live within city limits.

Meanwhile, the shelter workers have some criticism about the way the public acts, but they don't often have a chance to air their complaints. For instance, although they want to encourage people to bring their unwanted pets into the shelter instead of leaving them in an alley, they grow tired of the feeble excuses that pet owners give as reasons for getting rid of their cats and dogs.

"He's too playful," is a common reason, as is, "It's not housebroken." Others are, "It has fleas," "It sheds too much," "It has too many babies," and "It wants to be taken for walks all the time." One woman turned in a two-year-old dog because she was tired of looking at it. "This cat doesn't get along with my goldfish," was the actual reason given by another woman for getting rid of her pet.

Many people turn their pet in because it's grown too old, and others bring in litters of kittens and puppies saying, "We don't want these, but we did want our children to see the miracle of birth."

"I wonder how those pet owners would feel about taking their children into our euthanasia room," said a volunteer in one large shelter. "There they could see the tragedy of needless death. The problem is that there's not just an overpopulation of dogs and cats. There's an overpopulation of irresponsible dog and cat *owners*."

She might have added that it's these irresponsible owners who do much of the criticizing of the animal shelters. "Why don't they pick up these packs of strays?" they ask. "And what about all these barking dogs that ruin my sleep?" They also wonder why the people at the shelter must destroy so many young, healthy animals.

One shelter worker spoke for many of her co-workers when she said, "When a critic of the shelter puts on old clothes and spends just one week working in a shelter, dealing with terrified, vomiting pets and the excuses and criticisms of the public; when he spends ten to twelve hours a day hosing down runs, feeding animals, gaining their trust; when every day he has to select the twelve to twenty cats and dogs that have to be destroyed to make way for as many new ones; when he has killed his quota of perfectly healthy animals and disposed of their bodies; then he'll have the right to criticize us for not doing our job the way he thinks it should be done."

Perhaps at a poor shelter the employees don't care what people think about them. They may not even worry about how many careless pet owners there are. At a good shelter, however, the employees do care. They would like people to appreciate their hard work and their dedication. Even more, they would like people to become a lot more concerned about why that shelter remains so full of homeless animals, and why those animals are suffering even when they receive the best possible care.

The manager of one shelter told a reporter how he felt. "I'm proud of my shelter. It's one of the best, but it will never take the place of a good home. I see how these poor frightened creatures act when they are brought here. They whimper and they shake, and maybe even vomit from fright. But how different they act when someone adopts them. They leap into the air, lick their new owner's face, run in circles, and skid across the floor. Some of them are hysterical from happiness."

He paused for a moment. "Ask your readers how they would like to spend every day in a cage, when they hadn't done anything wrong. How would they feel when the only time they had any companionship was when someone fed them or hosed down their enclosure? Why don't *you* try it sometime? Then maybe you'd work a little harder to keep your pet from running loose on the streets."

6

Animal Problems, People Problems

THE ANIMAL CONTROL OFFICER spotted a small brown dog loping down a sidewalk in a quiet residential neighborhood. She stopped her truck, grabbed a length of rope, and positioned herself in the dog's path.

"Come here, pup," she crooned. "Come on over here."

The dog halted and sniffed the air. The voice he heard seemed gentle enough, but he evidently decided that there was something suspicious about a uniformed woman with a rope in her hand. Bounding through some ivy, he loped across the street. The officer followed, continuing to call, offering her hand for a sniff.

A few minutes later, the dog surrendered. With

his rump wagging sheepishly, and his eyes oozing trust, he allowed the officer to pat him on his head, and then to slip the rope leash around his neck.

When the dog was safely secured in one of the truck's six holding cages and the patrol resumed, the officer thought about her latest catch. No ID, she mused. That means there's almost no way to trace the owner. And that dog probably does have a home somewhere, because he's so healthy-looking, and so trusting.

She knew, as does every animal control officer, that corraling a "street smart" stray takes much more skill and patience than rounding up someone's usually-well-cared-for pet. An experienced street dog knows where there are holes in the hedges and which houses to run between to get quickly to the next street. He knows all the short cuts and all of the alleys that have dead ends. He remembers where there are holes and other hideouts that have small, hidden entrances.

"Wrong way Charley," was a clever and elusive dog who knew all of the one way streets in his area. Whenever he was being followed, he ran down one of these streets the wrong way. Unless traffic was very light, his frustrated pursuers had to take up the chase another day.

It doesn't take a stray long to learn how to spot a

uniformed human and a suspicious-looking vehicle long before he is spotted himself. One Texas animal control department changed the style of its uniforms and painted its patrol trucks a different color in order to fool the dogs. The expensive experiment was a failure.

"No matter what we did to disguise ourselves, I'd turn a street corner and some old dog a block away would look up, see me, and take off," said an experienced officer. "Most street dogs have a sixth sense that springs from a deep distrust of human beings. It's as if they have a built-in radar warning system."

New York City's huge population of strays has caused its dog catchers to become the most skilled in the country. They can rope a dog that's running thirty miles an hour, or one that's still in midair after jumping from a building. They know where the packs of feral dogs hang out, where they sleep, where they eat, and which ones will bite.

"THERE'S ONE," a driver will exclaim to his partner as he patrols a street. He then slams on the brakes, grabs a rope, and the pair will sprint toward the alley. The dog seems to sense that he's trapped as he darts first toward one man than toward the other. The rope is thrown and it catches between his jaws. A screaming, snarling sound comes from the animal's throat as the rope twists over his neck and is wrapped three times around his mouth. His hind legs try to grip the asphalt in his effort to escape, but his efforts are futile. He's on his way to the shelter and probably the euthanisation room.

The animal control officers often wish that every dog owner could ride with them for just one day. They want to tell everyone about how many animals are paying the price for human carelessness.

"DOG CATCHERS" often do much more than just catch dogs. They have formed human chains across swollen streams to rescue stranded cats. They have been scratched, bitten, butted, kicked, and gored by bulls, horses, deer, and innocent-looking but sharped-toothed seals. They are called out in the middle of the night and into fires, floods and storms to rescue animals. One of the most common, most dangerous, and yet most easily avoided animal emergency situation takes place in the middle of a busy highway. Sometimes the animal is there because his owner let him roam. At other times, he's there because he was being transported in the back of a pickup truck. It's not unusual for a dog to fall or to jump out of a pickup. In his panic, he either freezes or darts into the path of a car. Some people think a dog will be safe if he is tied to the truck. They are wrong, because the animal will probably strangle or be dragged to his death if it falls out. Many dogs are injured just by sliding around on the smooth floor of the truck bed. At the least, a dog's sensitive eyes, ears, or nose can be injured by dust or flying pebbles.

"There's no reason for anyone to put his dog on the back of a pickup," said one humane worker. "If there's no room for the animal in the cab, he should be left at home. There really ought to be laws against letting any animal ride in the back of an open truck."

Other emergency calls may involve ducks, roosters, skunks, raccoons, snakes, and horses. Almost every animal control officer has also been asked to pick up a lion, monkey, coyote, or a bear cub that someone tried to domesticate. Sooner or later, the owners of these exotic pets find that a wild creature is always a wild creature. Too often, by the time they discover this inescapable fact, the animal is no longer capable of living on its own in the wilderness. The zoos may have too many of that particular species already, so they can't take it in. The animal shelters usually aren't equipped to give it a permanent home either. Suddenly, there's no room anywhere for a creature that should have been left in its natural habitat in the first place. The only solution is to destroy it.

The life of an animal control person is filled with animal problems, but of course he expected such problems when he took the job. His life is also filled with people problems, most of which he probably *didn't* expect.

To many pet owners, he's the "bad guy." He's the one who impounds their dog when it bites someone who was teasing it. He's the one who sets a trap for their bird-eating cat. He issues the citations for the leash law violations and gets caught in the middle of pet-related neighborhood and family squabbles. He has to face the belligerent owner of a neglected animal and tell that angry man or woman that he's going to take their pet away.

If he doesn't show up in time to catch a snapping mongrel, he's called lazy and inattentive. If he picks up someone's prized Doberman, he's called an unfeeling monster who doesn't understand that dogs need their freedom. People waste his time by calling in false reports of animal emergencies. When he tries to catch a stray that's suspected of being rabid, the teenagers in the neighborhood call him names and hamper him in his work until the dangerous dog escapes. And when that dog bites someone, it's his fault because he let it get away.

Onlookers may pelt him with golf balls, stones, and whatever else they can lay their hands on. Someone may point a rifle at him just because he's wearing a uniform. They come at him with knives and fists, or break the windshield of his truck. One officer once tramped through a field full of poison ivy to catch a frightened, injured Irish setter. When he brought the animal back to his truck, he found that someone had opened the doors and released all of his previously captured dogs. One of them was a particularly vicious and possibly rabid fox terrier.

"He probably looked pitiful sitting in that holding cage," the officer said later. "But I wouldn't be surprised if the person who let him out is nursing some dog bite wounds right now. As for me, I got a three-week bout with the itch of poison ivy."

"No one seems to realize that what we're trying to do is protect both animals and people," he continued. "There are good reasons for the leash laws, but hardly anyone I come across understands why dogs can't run free. 'My dog is smart,' they say, 'He'd never do anything as dumb as getting in front of a moving car.'

"I wish everyone could see how many dead dogs I pick up every week, and most of them were killed by cars. 'You'll know you were wrong when a car knocks the life out of your pet,' I want to tell people. 'That animal has no business being on the street, not even once. You tell everyone how much you love him, but I don't believe it. If you really loved him, you'd keep him home where he belongs.' "

Other animals also suffer when dogs are allowed to run loose. In many suburban and rural areas, innocent-looking pets have been known to attack cattle, horses and wildlife. The attacks may start out as a simple game, but soon become serious as the dogs develop a feeling of power and a taste for blood. These same dogs may attack human beings. Their owners may never suspect what their seemingly gentle, thoroughly domesticated pets have been doing during their afternoon and evening absences.

PEOPLE WHO LET their dogs run loose are bad enough, but the owners who abandon their pets entirely are worse. An abandoned animal is a pitiful and often helpless creature, and a Pittsburgh, Pennsylvania, animal control officer was so moved by one of them that he wrote a letter that was published in the local newspaper. He hoped whoever had deserted the dog would read it and realize the pain he had caused.

"Your dog is dead," he wrote. "You know the black and white setter, the pregnant female, that you abandoned last summer around thirtieth and Hudson.

I thought you might want to know that she had her puppies in the cellar of a vacant house.

"Then she spent her time scrounging for food and running from people because she could no longer trust humans. Running wasn't easy because she had an injured right rear leg.

"I picked up two of her puppies, but the third crawled away, probably to starve to death. Very few puppies survive on their own. But mamma dog wasn't about to be captured, so she spent the rest of the summer scratching her mangy, flea-ridden body, searching for water when the temperature soared to 110, and trying to find food, while people were throwing rocks and cursing at her.

"As winter drew near, it was time for nature to take its course, and she was again with puppies. As she grew heavier, she couldn't run as fast, so she was cornered by an angry man in a yard. Someone shot your dog, but luckily she suffered for only a few minutes before she died. The problem you created for her and for the neighborhood was solved at last.

"Think awhile before you abandon another dog. You may believe that you're giving your pet a fighting chance to live a long life. What you're really doing is giving it a chance to fight fear and loneliness, thirst and starvation, disease and injuries, indifference and cruelty.

"If you no longer want your pet, bring it into the shelter. Yes, we might have to put it to sleep, but isn't a graceful, painless death better than the living hell that your black and white setter had to face every day?"

7

"It's Raining Cats and Dogs!"

T O EVERY MAN AND WOMAN who works in an animal shelter, the old phrase, "It's raining cats and dogs," is fast taking on a new and ominous meaning. In the United States, 170 puppies and kittens are born every minute. That number adds up to more than ten thousand per hour, or 90 million per year. The dog and cat population is, in fact, increasing three times faster than the human population.

Right now, there are 48 million families in this country, and many of them aren't interested in owning a pet. As a result, only about one out of every ten kittens and one out of every six puppies born today will be raised in a home. The situation will be worse tomorrow, and still worse next month and next year, unless steps are taken immediately to stop the excess breeding.

What will happen to the dogs and cats that don't find homes? About half of them will live on the streets, where, if they are lucky, they will survive for two years. During that time they will be hungry, sick, injured, and fearful. They will reproduce, nevertheless, so when they die they will leave plenty of strays to take their place.

The rest of the surplus dogs and cats will be surrendered to animal shelters. *Seventy-five to ninety percent of them will be euthanised.* Currently, the numbers add up to thirteen and a half million a year. That's a lot of killing. Is all of it necessary? The owners of some privately owned shelters say that it isn't. They claim that any dog or cat is adoptable if enough effort is made to find a home for it.

This statement gives people the impression that most other shelters are run by cruel and heartless men and women. But there's something that the owners of these super-humane shelters leave unsaid—the fact that since they aren't tax-supported, they can pick and choose among the animals they take in. The rest —the hopelessly ill, the aged, the badly crippled, the ugly, the emotionally disturbed—end up in public shelters where they must be put to sleep.

"We can't turn any animal away, but we can keep only so many of them in so many square feet," says Gib Rambo, who is the executive director of the

Fresno, California, animal shelter. "We don't like to get emotional about the subject of euthanasia. It's hard enough playing God with all the animals' lives without having all this misunderstanding about what we are able to do and what we are unable to do."

But if limited space is the answer, why not build more and larger shelters? The obvious answer to that commonly asked question is that there just isn't enough money available to feed and house every homeless animal for the rest of its natural life.

An even better answer is that what dogs and cats need are more and better homes, not more cages. Think about your own pet, or any other dog or cat you've ever seen. They may have acres in which to roam, but if they have a choice, where do they want to be? With *people,* of course. Human companionship is one of a dog's basic needs. While cats may seem more independent and self-sufficient, it's also one of theirs. Man himself has created and encouraged this dependency. Now man is putting these creatures into cages and allowing them only an occasional human contact, or abandoning them to the perils of life on the street. The punishment is a cruel and stressful one for an animal whose only crime was to be born.

Almost every caged dog or cat will eventually suffer emotional problems. Some of them will withdraw into themselves and spend their days huddled in a corner. Others will explode in rage and attack their cage mates or the kennel workers. Startling personality changes may occur within only a few days. For these unhappy creatures, a peaceful death is much better than constant confinement.

To make certain that such a death really is peaceful and painless, a great number of concerned people have spent a lot of time studying euthanasia methods. As a result, we've come a long way from the days when stray dogs were dropped, alive and struggling, into a vat of water, and when kittens were tied in a sack and dropped into a stream. There are now many methods available to animal shelters, but many of them are humane only under exactly the right conditions and sometimes even then, the animal may suffer unnecessarily.

Exposure to the fumes of carbon monoxide or carbon dioxide, the inhalation of chloroform or ether, and electrocution have all been tested. According to the HSUS euthanisation experts, they all come up short.

The high-altitude decompression chamber is a widely used, but highly controversial, method of euthanisation. The unwanted animals are placed in a chamber, and the air pressure inside is reduced by means of a vacuum pump. The lowered pressure results in a lack of oxygen, and the animals fall unconscious in less than a minute. The effect has been compared to the "blackouts" that are experienced by pilots who fly at high altitudes without the use of breathing equipment.

The HSUS doesn't consider the decompression chamber to be a humane way of killing animals. Their observers have seen evidence of pre-death internal hemorrhaging and convulsions in dogs and cats that have been euthanised in this way. Animals with respiratory problems show evidence of suffering extraordinary pain. Since many strays come into the shelter with lung infections, their deaths appear to be far from pain-free.

So far fourteen states have outlawed the use of the decompression chamber. These states are Arizona, Arkansas, California, Connecticut, Idaho, Kansas, Maryland, Massachusetts, Nevada, New York, Ohio, South Carolina, Tennessee, and Virginia. Humane workers managed to convince their legislators that the chamber can be a cruel euthanisation method even in the hands of caring, dedicated people. In the hands of people who don't care about animal suffering, it can be an instrument of unspeakable torture. An HSUS inspector was revolted when he saw one animal shelter's euthanisation process.

"Forty-two animals were forced to run through a narrow maze with brooms and shovels banging behind them. Those that fell down or tried to turn back were run down by the larger dogs. The feeling of panic from all those animals being crowded on top of each other in a chamber that could humanely handle only fifteen dogs was impossible to convey."

Many of the states that have outlawed the decompression chamber have replaced it with an injection method of euthanisation. The use of a hypodermic needle containing sodium pentobarbitol has many advantages, not the least of which is that it takes two people—one to hold and comfort the animal, the other to give the injection. Thus, the animal's last impression is of soft words and gentle hands and a pinprick. He loses consciousness within four or five seconds, and he's dead within twenty to thirty seconds.

There are drugs other than sodium pentobarbitol that are used to euthanise animals, but they can cause agonizing pain before death occurs. Thus, most humane workers support the use of sodium pentobarbitol.

The change from decompression chamber to the injection method of euthanisation also benefits the human beings who must associate with the animal victim.

"At least, if I bring a dog or cat to the shelter now, I know it will be put to death painlessly," is a typical citizen reaction.

"Sure, it was hard putting my old dog down," said a pet owner, "but he was in my arms until he died, and that made it easier for both of us. He didn't suffer at all."

The people who do the euthanising approve of the use of the needle, too. "It's harder in some ways," said a shelter worker. "With the chamber we were more removed from the killing. Now we have to face it directly because we're actually holding the animal when it dies. But we know it's better for the animal, and that's what counts. We can take more pride in doing an awful job in the best possible way."

No matter how easily death comes, the destruction of healthy dogs and cats is a hateful task. Very few shelter workers ever become completely hardened to the idea of killing young, healthy animals. Many of them develop their own emotional problems. They may have nightmares. They burst into tears at odd times and places. They feel guilty and apologetic for what they have to do. They must endure criticism, not only from the general public, but often from their own families and friends.

Some shelter managers now have therapy sessions in which the people who work in the euthanasia room talk about how they feel and how they cope with the stresses of their jobs. Every pet owner should listen to what they have to say.

"When a dog was going to be put to sleep," said one kennel worker, "I used to try to find an owner for him, but you know how people are. They let their pets run around. When the dogs get sick, they don't want to spend the money to make them well, so I'd get them back. It's irresponsible ownership, that's what it is. People just don't want to take care of their animals, and then we get the blame for what happens."

Another worker said that she spent her lunch hours bathing the animals and fluffing up their fur in the hope that they would look more attractive to the people who came into the shelter to adopt a pet. Other workers said that they took the animals out of their cages at night and played with them.

"Sure, it's hard playing with a litter of puppies that will probably be destroyed within a day or so," said one of them. "But then I think about some of the things I've seen happen to dogs on the street, and how they come in here hurt, starving, or worse, and I tell myself it's better this way. That's really the only way I can handle it."

"Of course, it gets to you," said a young man. "Some people say they get used to it, but they don't. But I think that euthanasia is necessary to relieve the suffering of unwanted animals. I think this as I see it being done, and I can usually deal with it."

A woman spoke for all of her coworkers when

she said, "It's difficult for me to go through the kennel and be the one who decides which will live and which will die. Who am I to play God and make such decisions? Who gave me that right? Then I remember that if I didn't care, and if I didn't love those unfortunate animals, who would? Mine may be the only kind hand they ever feel, the only soft voice they hear, the one and only human being who really did care.

"I remember one man who used to feel the same way I do. When he held the animal to be killed, he held it with care. The trouble is, he never forgot even one of them, and he felt more and more guilt. When some of his friends started calling him 'killer' as a joke, at first he was able to laugh. But later, he'd cry. He finally had to be transferred out of the euthanasia room.

"Right now, I'm at peace with my conscience, but there's still a constant feeling of death in my hands. I'll always know that life was there, and now it's gone. But, you know what? I've made up my mind to stop crying. Instead, I'm going to get mad, and I'm going to start telling people about what *really* happens to the dogs and cats they throw away."

MANY SHELTER WORKERS are now beginning to tell people about their anger. "We don't have a stray animal problem," they are saying. "What we have is a people problem. It's people who allow their pets to breed. It's people who don't keep them fenced in. It's people who dump their dogs and cats when they grow tired of them. It's people who refuse to understand the need for euthanisation and who call us killers."

Dr. John Kullberg, the executive director of the ASPCA, knows that his organization is often thought of as a slaughterhouse instead of a humane society. "But what can we do?" he asks. "Leave the strays on the streets? Build thousands of cages? Turn away unadoptable animals? Hire dogcatchers who look good to the public, but who can't catch dogs?"

Gib Rambo shares Dr. Kullberg's feelings. "It's unfortunate that we have to do the dirty work of the irresponsible pet owners," he says. "People look at us as if we're the culprits. We're sick and tired of being thought of as the black-hearted bad guys. Why don't pet owners stop letting their pets breed? If they did, we wouldn't have to worry about the best or worst euthanasia method, because mass euthanasia would be a thing of the past."

Phyllis Wright knows exactly how all of these people feel. She herself has ordered the killing of hundreds of young, healthy animals, and she has had to face the criticism of the public for her part in that killing. She, however, has come to grips with the most unpleasant part of her job.

"I can tell you one thing," she wrote in a news-letter, "I don't worry about any of the animals I've put to sleep. And I worry a great deal about the dogs and cats who have to spend their lives shut up in small cages or are left chained to the back porch day after day without affection or companionship. Being dead isn't a cruelty. Being half-alive is.

"We have the responsibility to release these animals from their suffering. We have the responsibility to make sure this release is as painless and as comfortable as possible. . . .

"We also have a responsibility to work toward a time when all pets will have dedicated, caring owners, and mass euthanasia is no longer needed."

8

Cat People and Dog People

PHYLLIS WRIGHT works full time as a director of HSUS. She travels all over the country to help educate pet owners and to ease the suffering of all animals.

Hettie Perry is also a full-time humane worker, but she seldom leaves the small southern California town in which she lives. She's often tired, and she's always short of money. Sometimes she's discouraged, because although she works twelve to fifteen hours a day, seven days a week, her job continues to get bigger instead of smaller.

Occasionally, like Phyllis Wright, Hettie is both sad and angry, because she lives constantly with first-hand evidence of the cruelty of animal overpopulation. She's the "Cat Lady" of El Monte, California.

As such, she has had as many as 400 feline "boarders" at one time, and averages from 250 to 300.

Hettie's career as a Cat Lady sneaked up on her. At first, all she did was to offer transportation to people who had no other way of getting their pets to the veterinarian's office. Soon, someone was asking her if she could find a home for a cat. The next request was to find homes for a litter of kittens, and then there were more adult cats. People began picking up strays and bringing them to Hettie's house.

As time passed, she found it more difficult to find homes for her cats, so her own home became more and more crowded. When she ran out of room, she moved to another house that had a larger yard. Now most of her cats are kept outside in sheltered, airy, room-sized cages, so there's no crowding. Her house still has a cat in every chair, under every table, and on every bed. Two or three of Hettie's friends come in every day to help her clean the litter boxes, distribute food and water, and give special care to any sick or injured animal. Each newcomer is given its protective shots as soon as it arrives, and if it's old enough to be spayed or neutered, Hettie arranges for the operation.

All of these tasks take a lot of time, but the most difficult job is finding good homes for her cats. "There's no point in placing them in poor homes,"

Hettie says. "Unless I feel certain that the cat will be well cared for, I'd just as soon keep it. Why adopt one out if it's just going to end up roaming the streets again?"

When Hettie isn't busy taking care of her cats, she's sorting through the aluminum cans, bottles, and newspapers that people donate to her. After loading them onto her truck, she drives to the various recycling centers. The money she earns from the salvage helps to buy food and pay medical expenses for the cats. Occasionally, people give her money, but there's never enough to get the extra things she needs.

"I want to run an electric line to the back yard," she says. "That way I'd have light so I could go through my salvage at night. But that's going to cost $200 and I don't have the money for it." She shrugs. "I suppose it will eventually come from somewhere. It seems that just when I need it the most, the money comes in."

Hettie is over seventy years old, but she can't retire. "Maybe I could someday, if only every cat owner would spay or neuter his pet. Then people like me would be out of business, except for an emergency now and then. And wouldn't that be great!"

She shakes her head and looks around her. "But it sure doesn't look as if that's going to happen soon, does it?"

* * *

ALMOST EVERY COMMUNITY has someone like Hettie living in it. Many people wonder whether or not these "cat people" or "dog people" are crazy, or at least a little "weird." Why else would they spend all of their time, energy, and money taking care of homeless animals? Perhaps Hettie herself agrees with them. Would a sane person do what she's doing? After all, there are established animal shelters in which people are getting paid to do what she does for nothing. All of those cats aren't *really* her responsibility, are they?

But when Hettie sees a cat that needs help, she doesn't worry about whether or not it's her responsibility. She doesn't have time to worry about what other people think of her. She doesn't feel as if she has to explain her way of life to anyone, because each time she saves a kitten's life, or places a grown cat in a good home, she knows that what she's doing is worthwhile.

"I sometimes wonder about those people who don't understand me," she says. "Are they the ones who allow their pets to have all those litters, and then abandon them or give them to someone who won't take care of them?"

JEAN MAHONEY has a beautiful home on a large plot of land in a small town in northern California. She could be spending her days watching television, or gardening, or lying in the sun beside her pool. She could be traveling in Europe with her husband, or playing bridge with her friends, but Jean has chosen to be a "Dog Lady."

Such an occupation means giving up those bridge games in order to take care of the poodles, spaniels, Airedales, Labradors, and other breeds of dogs that fill her house and yard. It means that her travels are limited to tracking down lost dogs, going around town to put up posters that describe someone's missing pet, or delivering a puppy to its new home. It means answering the telephone at any hour of the day or night, and then rushing out to take care of various pet emergencies.

Some of the dogs that Jean gets have been physically abused and some were struck by cars. Many of them are suffering emotional damage as well. They have lost their trust, their self-confidence, and their spirit. Sometimes Jean has to decide that the greatest kindness she could show an animal is to have it euthanised.

"It's not easy making that kind of decision," Jean says. "I don't do it unless I'm convinced that there's no hope the animal will ever be happy. It isn't fair to keep a miserable, hurting creature alive, but I do everything possible before I give up. I've worked with some dogs for several months before admitting to myself that they would never improve enough to be placed in a home."

Like Hettie Perry, Jean sees no end to the work in which she's involved. The number of surplus dogs keeps increasing, and sometimes Jean is angry.

"There's really no excuse for this dog overpopulation," she says. "We have an excellent spay and neuter program in this area. Why do people let their pets have litter after litter, then expect someone else to bear the pain and expense of caring for them and destroying them? It's just carelessness and thoughtlessness, that's all."

This anger is shared by other "one-person humane societies," such as the woman in Pasadena, California who happens to have the only fenced-in yard in her low-income neighborhood. People regularly drop their unwanted dogs inside her gate, even when they know that her small house is already filled with strays. Just a few miles away, more people dump their surplus dogs near a railroad crossing. A man who lives nearby gathers up these animals, has them spayed and neutered, and tries to find homes for them. One day he may have only three dogs. The next week, he may have over twenty. When his neighbors see him out walking several dogs at once, they look at each other and shrug. They don't understand why anyone would want to spend all of his spare time taking care of mongrels and mutts. Why not just call the people at the local shelter? Why does he take the animals into his home in the first place?

This man doesn't let such misunderstanding bother him. He's convinced that every hour he spends making an animal's life better is worthwhile. His feeling is shared by a campus guard at a large university in Southern California. He has built a large enclosure and collects all of the dogs and cats that people abandon on the campus. Occasionally he gets a donation from a student, but most of the food the dogs eat is bought with his own money. He estimates he has saved the lives of hundreds of dogs by placing them in good homes. In an eastern state there's a seventy-four-year-old man who has sold almost all of his acreage to get enough money to support the fifty to 100 dogs he has at any one time. Within the last four years, he has found homes for three thousand strays.

"All I want to do is place nice dogs with nice people," he said. "I won't let a dog go unless I know the home will be fine."

The problem is that he is painfully aware that for each stray that turns up at his doorstep, there are hundreds more roaming the streets. For each one he places with a good owner, hundreds more are being abused and neglected. For each hopelessly crippled or ill animal he has to put to sleep, hundreds more puppies and kittens are being born.

Every cat and dog person wonders why their fellow human beings allow this suffering to continue.

A wily stray often can elude his pursuers.

An apprehensive St. Bernard is taken into custody until its owner can be located.

Lassoing a turkey is just part of a day's work for an animal control officer. TERRY ANDRUES

The turkey, found walking down the middle of a city street, was later claimed by its owner.
TERRY ANDRUES

*An early, painful
death is the end of
the story for most
loose-running dogs.*
TERRY ANDRUES

This dog is lucky; it could have been hit by a car.
TERRY ANDRUES

PASADENA
HUMANE SOCIETY

Animal control people are prepared to rescue any animal that gets into trouble.

Dr. Michael Fox is director of the Institute for the Study of Animal Problems. He has written many books and articles that help people understand animal behavior.

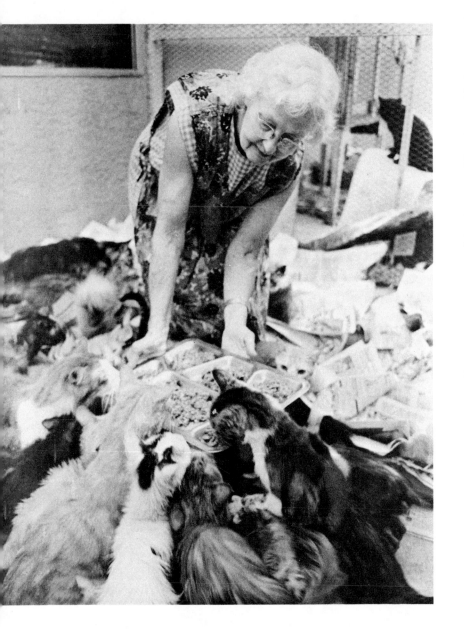

A boy and his dog are reunited. He has been told to keep his pet on a leash.

Hettie Perry has made a career of caring for unwanted cats. Just feeding them takes up a large part of her day.
TERRY ANDRUES

To Jean Mahoney, animal rescue is a twenty-four hour a day job. At the time this picture was taken, she and her husband Frank were caring for more than thirty formerly homeless dogs.

ROBERT POYNTER

A lucky kitten finds a home and older family members will make sure this little girl learns how to care for her new pet.

This new puppy owner promises to give his pet the best possible care.

9

"There's a Noise in My Chimney!"

STEVE, THE HUMANE OFFICER, fully understood the problems that occur because of dog and cat overpopulation because he faced those problems every time he came to work. He had once read that in his city the most common citizen complaints had to do with barking, biting, destructive dogs. All morning Steve had been following up on such complaints. It was already lunch time, but he couldn't stop. He had to investigate a dog-bite incident. He also had to see a woman who was hearing strange "animal noises" in her chimney. And there were always the long-standing complaints about the feral dogs that were roaming the west side of town. The mailmen in that area routinely carried several cans of dog repellent with them.

"The dog problem here is really out of control," one mailman had said to a newspaper reporter. "I spent four years in the Korean War and didn't get a scratch. I got all my battle scars on the streets of this town. But you know, I still feel sorrier for the dogs than I do for myself. Most of them were abandoned by their owners, and they're just doing what they have to do to survive."

Suddenly Steve received an emergency call about a hit-and-run dog accident nearby. He sped to the scene. When he arrived he saw an injured Irish setter mix lying near a trash-strewn curb. A thin, mangy-looking terrier was hovering over the injured animal. The terrier bared his teeth, stiffened his hind legs and growled a warning to Steve as he approached. Steve knew enough about dogs to take that warning seriously.

A crowd of people gathered to see how Steve was going to handle the situation. "Hey, dog man," called a teenage boy. "You gonna kill that hurt dog?"

"Not unless I have to," Steve replied. "I'll take him to the vet, and see what he can do. Looks like one of his legs might be broken."

"What about the little one?" a young girl asked. "You gonna shoot it?"

Steve reached into the cab of his truck and pulled out his "comealong," a tube of metal with a loop of leather on one end. "No reason to do that. I'll put it in my truck and take it back to the shelter so it won't get run over too."

"That terrier's a mean one," a man said. "He's been running around here for weeks, snapping at people."

Steve didn't believe the terrier was vicious. Frightened maybe, certainly confused, but not vicious. The small dog seemed more concerned about protecting his larger companion than he was about his own safety. He struggled and yelped when the loop of the comealong settled around his neck, then howled in anguish when Steve placed him in a holding cage.

More passersby stopped to watch as Steve wrapped a length of rope around the setter's mouth, then gently lifted him onto a blanket. Using the makeshift stretcher, he lifted the whimpering animal into the back of the truck. The terrier stopped howling when he saw that the larger dog wasn't going to be left behind.

Fifty minutes later the injured dog had been left at an animal hospital, and the terrier had been placed in the observation area of the shelter along with all the other newcomers. Steve was back on his rounds, and standing outside the fence that bordered the dirt yard of a small house. He was facing a pony-sized

Great Dane and its belligerent owner.

"Sure, Duke bit the guy," said the owner, "but my dog doesn't like to be teased. That guy stuck his face right in front of Duke's mouth and pretended he was going to take his bone away from him. He got just what he deserved."

It wasn't Steve's job to judge who was at fault, although he knew that most dog bites could be prevented if people would just use common sense. Just last week someone had tried to take a newborn puppy away from its mother and had been bitten.

Right now it was Steve's job to get the dog into the shelter for rabies observation. "I'm sorry, but Duke has to be quarantined for eight days," he said. "It's the law. Do you want me to take him in, or will you do it?"

"Duke's not going to like being locked up," the young man muttered. "But as long as it has to be done, I'd just as soon bring him in myself."

Steve suppressed a sigh of relief. Several people had gathered to watch the confrontation, and he felt the hostility in the air. "Thanks," he said. "Have Duke at the shelter by four this afternoon. And don't worry about him. He'll be well-treated."

As he drove to his next destination, Steve thought about the two dogs that he had picked up earlier. He shook his head to clear away the memory of the haunted look in the terrier's eyes. Someone had hurt that dog. Someone was responsible for his predicament. And, as usual, it was the dog that was paying for some human's neglect. The familiar anger filled Steve's chest.

His next job worsened his mood. Two Doberman pinschers had been left tied in a yard that was filled with dog droppings, broken glass, and rusty cans. Their dull coats were caked with their own filth, and open sores covered their emaciated bodies. Steve was touched by the sight of the male Dobie trying to keep a horde of flies from settling on his weaker female companion. When he wasn't snapping at the insects, he was licking at a sore on her back and trying to comfort her.

There was a pail of scummy water in the yard, but neither dog could reach it because their leashes were tangled in a bush. According to the person who had called the shelter, the people who lived at this address hadn't been home for at least three days.

The dogs were too tired and too sick to put up much of a fight. Within ten minutes Steve had them safely stored in the back of his truck. He thought for a moment before he started the engine. The Dobies needed medical attention, but a delay of thirty minutes or so wouldn't make any difference in their condition. His next stop was on the way to the animal hospital, so he might as well take care of it.

A few minutes later he stopped in front of an old two-story house. A woman met Steve at the door. "I'm glad you're here," she said. "Can't imagine what's in my chimney, but about eight this morning, I started hearing scrabbling noises."

Steve reached into the chimney with his gloved hand. Sure enough, there was something there. He tugged at what seemed to be a paw, but whatever it was seemed to be stuck. After grasping what felt like a tail, Steve yanked as hard as he could. A few seconds later, a soot-covered four-foot lizard was lying on the hearth.

As Steve turned to the woman, he expected to see her fall to the floor in a faint. Instead, she screamed joyfully. "George! I was hoping that was you. Why did you hide from me?"

Steve grinned as he walked back to his truck. Occasionally, in the midst of all of the dead-animal, abused-animal, and stray-animal calls, something like this came along. What a good feeling it was to be able to laugh at the outcome of a job. He remembered the time that someone had reported a dead bird on the freeway. When he had responded to that call, he had found a plucked and frozen twenty-four-pound turkey lying on the shoulder of an off ramp. At first Steve had laughed at the incident, but later he felt a resentment toward the unknown practical joker who had taken up his valuable time with a prank, and toward all the people who called in false stories of animal emergencies.

As he climbed into his truck after retrieving the lizard, Steve again found himself thinking about the terrier that he had picked up earlier. What's so special about that dog? he wondered. Why can't I just forget about it? I can't let myself worry about any of these strays. I can't let them get to me. If I do, I'll have to quit this job.

ONE WEEK LATER, Steve attached a leash to the terrier's collar and led him to his car. He had officially adopted the stray. As he thought about all the other animals in the shelter, he felt guilty for leaving them behind. But after all, he decided, I can't save *all* of them. That shouldn't stop me from saving *one* of them.

He patted his newly acquired pet. "You and I are going to get along just fine," he murmured when he felt the dog shrink from his touch. "You don't ever have to be afraid again."

The terrier looked at Steve, apprehension filling his eyes. Steve knew he was going to have to work hard to gain the dog's trust, but he was willing to do whatever was necessary. This was one animal that wasn't going to end up back on the streets or in the shelter.

"Muggsy," he said. "That'll be your name—Muggsy."

The dog looked up at him and stopped shivering. At this moment his stomach was full, and he was warm, and no one was shaking a fist or throwing a rock at him. For a dog that had lived from moment to moment on the dangerous streets of the city, perhaps those things were enough to still his fear of this stranger. He edged closer to Steve and tentatively licked his hand.

10

Some Happy Endings

S EVERAL YEARS AGO an ordinary-looking stray dog chose as his territory the brush-covered land beside a certain stretch of highway in northern California. As time passed, the many truckers who regularly traveled that route came to regard this scruffy little terrier as something more than just another stray. They named him Whitey and admired his independent attitude and his mischievous and playful spirit. When they were in the area, they looked forward to pulling their big rigs onto the shoulder of the road, then calling to their unofficially adopted pet. Whitey always responded, because he knew that the humans brought food with them.

Whitey dined well—even better than some dogs that live in homes. He gulped down bologna sandwiches and pieces of chicken and roast beef. Occasionally, he gnawed on a steak bone that still had tender slivers of meat clinging to it. His tail wagged as

he showed his gratitude, but he refused to allow anyone to touch him. Many of the truckers wanted to
take him home, but their efforts to catch him were
futile.

Whitey spent most of his time resting or watching the traffic, or playing with the scraps of an old
tire. He seemed to be content with his solitary life.
He also appeared to be able to avoid the hazards of
living just a few yards away from a constant flow of
speeding cars and trucks. But one day his luck ran
out. Two years after he had been adopted by the
truckers, Whitey was crushed under the wheels of
a car.

CB radios carried the news of his death from one
big wheeler to another. Whitey was buried in a sheltered spot just off the highway, but the people who
had befriended him wanted to do more. They com-
memorated the little stray dog by erecting an en-
graved white stone monument by the side of the road.

Compared to most strays, Whitey lived well. For
the last two years of his life, at least, he was fed regularly, and his death came quickly. Almost all of the
stray dogs and cats that roam our streets and alleys
hardly ever know the good feeling that comes from
having a full stomach and being loved. Occasionally,
however, there is a happy ending to the story of one
of them.

One such story is that of the "iceplant dog." He

was a black shepherd-collie mix who used to spend most of each day sitting on a slope that overlooked a busy highway in northern California. As the days grew into weeks and he grew thin, the local residents began talking about him. They gave him the name of the iceplant dog because of the iceplants that grew on that hill.

Barbara Gordon was one of those residents, and she was more concerned about the dog than most of her friends. She wondered why he had chosen such a spot as his solitary lookout. Maybe he enjoyed the view of the swiftly flowing stream of traffic. Barbara thought it was probably because he was waiting for his former owner, someone who had abandoned him there.

Barbara knew that the past of this lonely, starving creature would remain a mystery, but his future seemed predictable—almost inevitable. He would either starve, die from a disease, or dart onto the highway and be crushed under the wheels of a car or truck.

Barbara had seen the local animal control officers trying to capture the dog. They had attempted to lure him with food and with coaxing words. They had tried to throw a net over him and to lasso him with a rope, but none of their tricks had worked. The wily iceplant dog always turned and ran in the opposite direction when any human drew close. He had evidently lost all of his faith in people.

Many of the nearby residents had also tried to catch the dog, but they all gave up after a few days. Barbara finally decided to capture the stray herself. Once the decision was made, nothing could stop her. Two weeks passed, and she was still trying.

"I can't give up," she told her friends when they told her she'd never succeed. "Maybe you're right, but as long as I know he's there and that I might be able to save his life, then I have to keep trying. I have to do *something*."

That "something" included leaving the warmth of her home in drenching rainstorms to carry food to the dog at the same time every afternoon. It included spending hours kneeling just a few yards away from where he sat, talking to him, hoping that he would forget his fear long enough to approach her. It included neglecting her work and her friends, because the life of a strange dog had suddenly become more important than they were.

A month passed before the dog began to respond to Barbara's voice and her outstretched hand. One day he crept close enough to grab a piece of meat from her hand, but then he turned and ran. Barbara decided it was time to ask for help.

The next morning, while she held the dog's attention, two animal control officers came up on the other side of the slope. By the time the dog realized what was happening, the net was settling over his back. Surprisingly, he didn't struggle. His quick surrender caused Barbara to believe that he welcomed his capture.

She was right. After only a few days in Barbara's home, the iceplant dog seemed happy to put his days as a stray behind him. He was soon responding to his new name of Tucker and was zealously guarding Barbara's yard from intruders.

THE PEOPLE at the local shelter were glad to hear about the happy ending to the iceplant dog's story. Every life saved, every stray rescued, is a victory for them. They know, of course, that there are many more unhappy endings than happy, but they force themselves to remain optimistic about the fate of the animals in their care. They try not to think about how many dogs and cats are scheduled to die in the euthanasia room. They ask, instead, "Who's going to find a home today?" and "Which one will be adopted?"

When an animal has endured an unusually severe or prolonged period of pain and neglect, there's even more reason to celebrate a happy ending to its story. Smiley was a Beagle who suffered for the first seven years of her life. Her owner had put a flea collar around her neck when she was a small puppy. As she grew, the collar hadn't been removed or expanded. When Smiley was brought into the shelter by a sympathetic neighbor, the band of plastic was buried three-fourths of an inch into her flesh. The dog's entire neck was an open wound.

The collar was removed, but upon closer examination the veterinarian discovered several bullets in Smiley's body. The wounds had never been treated. Only a strong will to survive had kept this dog alive. Her constant good humor belied the fact that she must have been in constant pain for most of her life.

Smiley eventually recovered completely and was placed in a good home. Her story made the shelter workers believe, at least for a while, that they have the most satisfying job in the world.

Tom Jenson likes to tell his friends that he didn't adopt his dog. Instead, his dog adopted him. He had been sitting on his front porch enjoying the coolness of the evening after a hot Fourth of July afternoon. The sound of fireworks punctuated the air, and occasionally there was a streak of red, blue, or gold in the sky as some celebrant fired a rocket.

To Tom, the scene was a relaxing one, and he

was growing drowsy. He was suddenly startled into wakefulness as a huge white dog galloped across his yard and through his open front door.

After waiting a few minutes, hoping in vain that the dog would come out, Tom cautiously entered the house. He found the animal huddled behind a couch. Its mouth was dripping saliva and its eyes were glazed. For a moment, Tom thought it might be rabid, but then he realized that it was actually in a state of terror. The fireworks, he thought. He had read how the sharp noises affect some dogs.

Besides being panic-stricken, the dog was in a generally poor condition. It was thin, its coat was dull and patchy, its stomach was covered with a rash, and the pads on its feet were torn and bleeding. Tom knew that this dog had been on its own for a long time, but there was still a chance that someone was looking for it. The next day he put an advertisement in the lost and found column of the newspaper.

After waiting a week for a response, Tom decided that the dog was his. He gave his new pet the name of Harley.

The following winter, Tom and Harley went for a hike in the nearby mountains. On the way down a steep trail Tom slipped and injured his back when he landed on the dry stream bed below. He found that he was unable to move. That night the temperature dropped to freezing, and Tom wondered how long he could survive without heat.

His problem was solved when Harley draped himself over his master's body. The dog's warmth probably saved Tom's life.

When the sun rose the following morning, Harley left Tom's side and went to find help. He reappeared an hour later with two men. By noon Tom was resting in a hospital, while Harley was having his picture taken by newspaper photographers. The evening paper carried the story of the stray dog who had repaid a man for giving him a home by saving that man's life.

DOGS HAVE SAVED many human lives, and local newspapers often carry such stories. Some dogs get publicity in other ways. Perhaps they are skilled at catching Frisbees, or were selected to be the local baseball team's mascot. A few cats and dogs are so unusual looking or have such good personalities that they are chosen to appear on television or in the movies. Morris, the cat who became famous by appearing in cat food commercials, was found by an animal talent scout in a humane society shelter near Chicago. He was adopted just twenty minutes before his scheduled euthanisation.

Johnny, the dog that stars in the "Here's Boomer" television series, was actually on a cart and being rolled into a euthanasia room when he was spotted by the person who adopted him. His life was saved by a mere few seconds.

Another famous dog also had only a short time to live when he was spotted by a talent scout. No one knows much about his life before he was picked up by an ASPCA driver. He had come to the humane society's attention because someone had complained about a medium-sized snapping mongrel that was disturbing the neighborhood.

The driver who responded to the call knew that this stray was more of a danger to himself than to people. As he led the fearful and confused animal into the shelter, he saw that its legs were trembling.

When the stray was placed in a cage with two other dogs, he immediately retreated to the furthest corner and stayed there. He refused to eat and took only a few laps of water when his thirst forced him to creep to the water dish. Even when he slept, his emotional state was evident. He twitched and shivered and moaned, as in his dreams he relived some of the terrible experiences he had suffered during his short life.

The humane workers believed that this pitiful creature would never be adopted. As soon as the required legal waiting period was over, he would be euthanised.

On the day before he was to be destroyed, a

young man came into the shelter. He was looking for a certain kind of dog to fill a very special job. As he walked up and down the aisles, he paused to look first at one animal, then at another. That one was too small, this other too big. A third was a possibility. The man realized what a difficult decision it was going to be. There were so many appealing dogs, and he could choose only one.

Eventually, the young man stood in front of the cage that held the brown mongrel. He noticed the matted coat, and the way his ribs stuck out along its sides. He saw the scars that had been left from a dog fight. He saw the hopelessness in its eyes.

But he saw something else in those eyes. They were large, and the color of melting chocolate. There was intelligence in them, and they also held a very special warmth. Those unforgettable eyes made the young man ignore the dog's obvious faults.

This is the one, he decided. I just hope my boss agrees with me.

He looked at his watch. It was almost time for the shelter to close for the day, and he couldn't take the dog without his boss's approval. A sense of desperation crept over him when he talked to the shelter manager and found that the mongrel was to be destroyed early the following morning.

"Please hold onto him for me," the man pleaded.

"I'm almost sure he's the one we want."

"I'll try," the manager said. "Come back at eight o'clock tomorrow morning—as soon as we open."

The next day at the time the mongrel had been scheduled to die, he was being placed in the arms of his new owner. A few months later, this "sorry-looking mutt" was standing beside a young girl on a Broadway stage and listening to round after round of applause.

As the canine star of "Annie," Sandy became a celebrity overnight. He had his picture taken when he visited the White House and shook hands with President Jimmy Carter, and his autobiography was published. Sandy had risen from a miserable life in the gutters and alleys of New York City to stardom and fame.

Even better, however, he had found a home with the young man who had seen a certain quality buried deep in a homely mongrel's big brown eyes.

11

A Beloved Pet
or
a Disposable Object?

PUBLICITY certainly helped advance the careers of both Morris the cat, and Sandy the dog. Publicity can also help to provide happy endings to the stories of more ordinary stray animals. Recently, a young fox terrier was rescued from a busy street in downtown Washington, D.C. A photographer happened to be on the scene and he took a picture of the dog. An illustrated story of the incident appeared in the evening edition of the newspaper. The next day the shelter was flooded with calls from people who wanted to adopt that one stray animal.

"How can you even think about putting that adorable puppy to sleep?" the shelter workers were asked.

No one likes a stray animal story with a happy ending more than Phyllis Wright does, but she wondered why all of those animal lovers didn't rush to the shelter to adopt some of the dogs and cats that weren't lucky enough to get their stories in the newspaper.

"I am constantly amazed by reporters who exploit the plight of a single animal, while completely ignoring the millions that are destroyed annually in our country's shelters," she said.

The problem is, of course, that most people don't want to think about millions of homeless animals. The situation is so overwhelming they feel that nothing can be done about it. They can, however, look at just *one* sad-eyed dog or cat and believe that there's hope for saving its life. Many animal shelters and humane societies have a prospective "Adoptee of the Week," a dog or cat that is due to be euthanised. An appealing picture of the doomed animal is published in the local newspaper. As a result, that lucky dog or cat will probably find a home. If the shelter had published a group picture of *all* the animals that were available, it's doubtful that any of them would be adopted.

The same kind of thinking seems to apply when people surrender their pets to a shelter. No one wants to face the fact that his unwanted, but adorable pet, will be competing with countless other adorable creatures. Perhaps this unwillingness to face the truth keeps pet owners from feeling guilty and from taking full responsibility for their actions and for the puppies and kittens they have allowed to be born.

One of the most difficult jobs that humane workers have is getting careless pet owners to face the truth —that *they* are the ones who are causing the dog and cat overpopulation problem. If each single pet owner took the proper care of his dog or cat, there would eventually be no surplus animals. There would be no more thousands of pets and strays dying under the wheels of cars every year. There would be no need to have mass euthanisations. Animal shelters could shelter animals, not destroy them. Humane workers could feel a sense of joy and accomplishment, instead of guilt and despair.

Michael Fox is a veterinarian who is very active in humane work. In his speeches and his articles, he stresses the idea of pet "stewardship," instead of pet "ownership."

"If we believe that we are morally responsible for the care of animals," he says, "and if animals do indeed have rights, then we should no longer speak of the 'ownership' of a cat or a dog. We should speak, instead, of 'responsible stewardship.' "

In other words, a pet shouldn't be considered our personal property in the same sense that a football, or a bicycle, or a piece of furniture is. A dog can't be placed on a shelf, or a cat stored in a garage when someone tires of it. Yet many people do seem to think of pets as disposable objects. When New York City's "scoop law" went into effect a few years ago, hundreds of dogs were suddenly left in parks and alleys or surrendered to animal shelters. Evidently, the small task of cleaning up a dog's waste on a public street was too much to ask of these pet owners.

Maybe you don't have a pet, but you may be thinking about how much fun you could have with a frisky puppy, or a cuddly kitten. The people at your local animal shelter certainly wouldn't want to deny you the pleasures of owning a pet, or an animal the security of a good home. They do wonder, however, how long that dog or cat will remain in your home when you find out that along with the fun, there's work and inconvenience. Kittens claw furniture, rugs, and draperies, and their litter boxes have to be cleaned every day. Puppies dig, chew, whine, and yap. A lonely newcomer may whimper or howl all night and disturb your sleep. Until it's housebroken, you'll find puddles and piles in unexpected places.

Life with your pet will become easier as time passes, but he'll still have to be exercised, groomed, watered, and fed for the rest of his life. He'll need licenses, shots, and medical care for ten to fourteen years. Are you and your family going to grow tired of the expense and responsibility? A pet deserves to have a good steward. Are you capable of being one?

Responsible pet stewardship begins with picking out the right pet. An animal shelter or a volunteer humane organization is the best place to "shop" for it. You'll find almost any type and size of dog or cat, and the cost will be small. A second choice is a breeder with a long-established excellent reputation. *Don't go to a pet store to buy a puppy or kitten.* An owner of such a business usually cares about nothing except making a sale. He isn't concerned about how you're going to get along with your new pet.

There's another reason for not going to a pet store to get a dog or cat. Many such stores obtain their puppies from what are known as "puppy mills." A puppy mill is just that—a place where female dogs are bred again and again so the owner can make money. The animals often have to live in small, dirty cages and when their usefulness is over, they're abandoned. The puppies are usually represented as purebreds, but more often than not their papers are fictitious.

Pups that are born into a puppy mill situation are usually mistreated, neglected, and then shipped under miserable conditions over hundreds of miles. The result is often a nervous, sick animal with a poor background. Such a dog makes an unsatisfactory pet.

If you want a good all-round family pet, get a

mongrel. Purebreds are beautiful dogs that can satisfy a human's vanity, but they are often delicate and "jumpy" creatures that are prone to illness. The HSUS would like to see more healthy, good-natured dogs rather than dogs that are bred just for show.

If you already own a pet, what kind of steward are you? Is your dog or cat fed regularly, and does he always have plenty of fresh water? Has he had all of his protective shots? Is he sheltered from the heat of summer and the cold of winter?

Is your dog trained to sit, heel, and stay? A trained dog is much less likely to be a nuisance or a danger to anyone, and obedience to these three simple commands can save his life in an emergency situation. Your local animal shelter, humane society, or city recreation department may offer low-cost obedience lessons. If not, your library probably has several good books on do-it-yourself dog training.

Do you allow your dog to run loose because you think he needs a lot of room in which to exercise? Actually an area of ten by twenty feet is big enough for even a St. Bernard or a Great Dane, as long as he gets enough attention and is taken out for a walk every day. When you're walking your dog, be sure to use a leash. A leash is your pet's lifeline.

Keeping your dog leashed or at home can save you money, because you won't be paying fines for violating leash laws and to retrieve him from the animal shelter. You might also be saved from paying veterinarian bills that result from your pet being hit by a car or from catching various diseases from strange dogs that he meets.

A dog should be fenced in, not tied up. A tied dog is in danger of being injured because of choking or tangling. A tied dog is also often a barking dog, and a nuisance to you and to your neighbors.

If you *must* tie your pet for any length of time, install a wire from a point on your house to a tree or a pole. Put a metal ring on the wire and fasten one end of a dog chain onto the ring and the other to your dog's collar. Make sure there are no bushes in which he can become entangled, and that he can't jump off or over anything and be hanged.

It's expensive to fence in a large yard, so you might want to consider fencing in just a small portion of it for your dog. Big department stores such as Sears sell portable dog runs, which will save you from having to put up any fence at all.

Check your fence regularly for holes, missing boards, and loose gate latches. Look under it for signs of digging.

Contrary to what most people think, cats don't need to prowl any more than dogs do. They can also be leash-trained if you start when they're young. If your cat is spayed or neutered, he will usually be content to stay in your house as long as he has a litter box, a scratching post, and a window through which he can look out upon the world. Cats have good imaginations. If they can see birds through a pane of glass, they can pretend they are catching them. They can thus have all the fun of the hunt without any of the harm.

Another misconception about cats is that they are fully capable of taking care of themselves. Many farmers believe that a cat needs only a barn for shelter and a daily bowl of milk. They think that any cat can hunt mice and thus furnish himself with an adequate diet.

The truth is that a so-called "barn cat" often suffers just as much as a stray cat in the city. Their population may double each spring because of uncontrolled breeding, but during the summer twenty-five percent of them will be killed by farm machinery and by cars. In the winter more will die because of starvation and exposure to freezing weather. The survivors suffer from disease, hunger, and parasites.

Dogs and cats that live away from the crowded centers of cities have another big problem—that of foxtails. This dangerous plant has been called the "weed that kills." If you see your dog or cat rubbing his eyes or squinting, pawing at his ears or shaking his head more than usual, he may have encountered a fox-tail's sharp pointed barbs. These painful barbs can enter any body opening, such as the rectum or the nose, and they can become buried in the skin, and be-tween the toes. Eventually, they can work their way into an internal organ and cause an agonizing death.

Keep your pet away from fields, yards, and va-cant lots that contain foxtails. If he shows symptoms such as rubbing, biting, and scratching a particular part of his body, rush him to a veterinarian.

Of course, any time your pet acts as if he's in pain, or refuses to eat for several days in a row, or shows other signs of illness for more than a day or two, you should take him to the veterinarian.

Your dog or cat should always wear a collar with an attached identification tag that bears your address and telephone number. An ID tag is the best possible loss insurance you can buy for your pet. It acts as a lost animal's "voice." If you have a cat, ask the clerk at the pet store or animal shelter about the "break-away" collar. It's designed to prevent climbing ani-mals from getting caught in trees and on fences.

Finally, your dog or cat should be spayed or neu-tered. Neutering will help make your male cat less likely to roam and to fight with other animals. It also helps to prevent urinary tract infections. Spaying your female dog or cat helps to prevent certain forms of cancer as it grows older. Contrary to what you may have heard, this operation is painless and simple, and it won't make your pet fat or lazy. Only overeating and lack of exercise will do that.

Of course, the main benefit of spaying and neutering is that you won't end up with any unwanted litters. In fact, *making certain that your pet has this operation is the one most important contribution you can make toward solving the dog and cat overpopulation problem*. Preventing just one litter from being born can prevent an untold amount of misery.

Don't excuse yourself by saying that you always find homes for the babies that your pet produces. Each animal that you place will cause another animal in your local shelter to remain unadopted.

And what would you find if you were to check up on all of those puppies and kittens that you so casually give away? You'd discover that, within a year or two, many of them would be lost, abandoned, dead, or in an animal shelter. You'd find that most of the surviving females had had litters of their own, and that those animals will soon be breeding also. Your female dog, having just one litter of four pups a year, can produce, with the help of her female offspring, over *four thousand* puppies in seven years. Can you find homes for all of them? Of course you can't, and neither can anyone else.

Cats are able to breed several times a year, instead of only twice as dogs can. During the spring and summer months, many large animal shelters have received up to three hundred cats in a single day. Animal control people find kittens that were left in sealed cardboard cartons, wrapped in newspaper and stuffed in trash cans, shut up in telephone booths and in empty apartments, and dumped in parked cars. Not one of these animals should have been born.

All of the rules of responsible pet stewardship can be summarized in just a few words. Your dog or cat doesn't need unbounded freedom to roam. It doesn't need freedom from rules and restrictions. It doesn't need babies in order to be happy.

What it does need is an ID tag, food, water, shelter, and attention. Any good steward knows that's a small price to pay for a pet's loyalty, companionship, and love.

12

"Where, Oh Where Can He Be?"

No one is perfect. Maybe one of your friends left your gate open. Or maybe *you* did. Perhaps your dog finally managed to dig a hole under the fence. It doesn't make any difference how he got away. Your dog is gone, and you can't assume he'll find his way back by himself. The sooner you start looking for him, the better.

Start immediately by thoroughly searching the area from which he disappeared. Walk around the block calling his name. If he was last seen at home, tell your neighbors that your dog is missing, and enlist the aid of the mailman and other delivery people. Ask your parents to help you. Many pets come out of hiding when they hear the family car passing by.

If you don't find him right away, continue your

search in the early morning and in the evening. At those times there is usually less noise from traffic, and your voice will carry better as you call your pet's name. You, on the other hand, will be better able to hear an answering bark or meow.

Take the time to investigate any place that could provide shelter, such as ditches, holes, and abandoned buildings. An injured animal will try to find a refuge.

If a day passes, and your pet is still gone, make some posters with your telephone number and a brief description of your dog or cat. Tack them onto posts and poles near schools, supermarkets, and any other places where people gather.

Place an advertisement in the lost and found column of your newspaper. Check the "found" ads every day.

Report your loss to the animal shelter, but remember that the people who work there are looking after dozens, even hundreds, of animals. You can't depend on them to spot one particular cat or dog when it comes in. Visit the shelter in person every two or three days, and call your pet's name as you walk up and down the aisles. Be sure to check the section that houses the sick and injured animals.

If there's a "pet finder" group in your area, report your loss to it. There may be a small fee for this service, but it's worth it. These groups have contacts with many animal shelters in an extended area, and some have computerized lists of dogs and cats that have been lost or found.

The most important thing to remember in a search for a lost pet is DON'T GIVE UP! Somewhere your pet is waiting for you to find him. Many pets have been returned to their homes weeks or even months after they became lost. Most of these successes occurred because their owners refused to stop looking.

Another important point—your pet has a hundred percent better chance of being returned to you if it's wearing an ID tag. This tag says more than just who the animal belongs to. It says that this animal has a home, and that someone cares about it and wants it back. Whoever finds a tagged dog or cat usually makes the effort to locate its owner.

Don't neglect getting a tag because you are certain that your dog will never get out of your yard. Animal shelters take in many pets whose owners thought they were securely fenced in. Fences and walls can be destroyed by a fire, flood, or an earthquake. Every Fourth of July close to one out of ten dogs panics at the sound of fireworks. Some of them go into a state of shock or hysteria during which they knock down strong enclosures or leap over tall fences.

After running until they're exhausted, they find themselves in unfamiliar territory and can't find their way back home.

Knowing the hazards of this holiday, a smart dog owner will keep his pet in the house until things quiet down.

What should you do when it's not your pet, but someone else's pet that's lost? Maybe a strange dog just turned up at your door, or there's been a scrawny little kitten hanging around the school grounds. Don't ignore it and hope it will go away. Here's your chance to help a frightened animal, and perhaps reunite a valued pet with its distraught owner.

You should, of course, use caution when approaching any animal that you don't know. If a dog is snapping or snarling, or a cat is spitting and daring you to touch him, you should leave it alone and call the animal control department or a humane society. If you must handle an injured animal, wear a jacket and a pair of heavy gloves, because it might bite.

If the animal is tame and nonthreatening, see if it's wearing an ID tag. If it is, your job is simple. Just confine it and telephone its owner.

If there's no tag, confine the animal, and call an animal control officer. The shelter is one of the first places a pet owner will look for a missing cat or dog. If you keep it in your home while you try to find out where it belongs, you might rob someone of a chance to find his pet.

If you must take care of the lost animal for more than an hour or two, write your name and telephone number on a piece of adhesive tape, then stick the tape on a collar or on a length of rope and put it around the animal's neck. This makeshift ID will enable the dog or cat to be returned to you if it escapes. It's a frustrating experience to find an animal, locate its owner, then lose the animal before it can be claimed.

There's a waiting period at almost all shelters, during which no healthy animal can be adopted or destroyed. Find out how long that waiting period is and use it to hang up "Found" posters, to place a "Found" ad in the newspaper, and to check out the animals that have been advertised as lost. Many newspapers don't charge for placing "Found" ads.

IF ANIMAL SHELTERS weren't so full of unwanted strays, the people who work in them could spend more time reuniting lost pets with their owners. As the situation is now, they can return only the pets that have ID tags. Sometimes, because of a lack of time, even this job is difficult. People move and don't have the address on the tag changed. They may be away from home on vacation, so several telephone calls have to be made. If you can help return just one lost cat or dog to its owner, you will have done an important deed. You will have aided your local animal shelter in its work. You will have made the animal's owner happy. Best of all, you will have saved a dog or cat from a terrifying existence on the streets.

13

More Than a Million Dog Bites

The *Animals are Crying* is the name of a film that's used by humane workers in their educational programs. It depicts in haunting detail the suffering that's endured by homeless cats and dogs. No one who sees this movie can easily forget the hungry, sick, and hopeless creatures that roam our streets.

There's another side to the stray animal problem, however, and it's one that some animal lovers tend to ignore. *People* are also suffering because of animal overpopulation. Consider, for instance, the one million, five hundred thousand men, women, and children who are bitten by dogs in our country every year. Most of these injuries are inflicted by family pets, but in New York City, stray dogs regularly attack children to grab lunches they are carrying to school. In Chicago, there are elderly men and women who are more afraid of being attacked by a dog than by a mugger.

Unleashed and stray dogs and cats knock over trash cans and tear open garbage bags, scattering litter that attracts disease-carrying flies and rodents. They deposit their own solid and liquid waste on playgrounds and sidewalks. Children then play in these areas and after touching the dirt and sand put their fingers in their mouths. Some parasites that get into their bodies may only make them slightly ill. Others may cause them to go blind, or to die.

In the United States one million dogs and cats are killed by cars every year. Thousands of human beings may also be killed or injured when they swerve their cars to avoid hitting animals. The ASPCA once reported a forty-car-reaction collision that extended for three miles and caused eleven serious injuries and $10,000 worth of damage. The accident began when the lead driver suddenly changed lanes so he wouldn't hit a dog that had darted into the street.

Loose dogs pursue and kill millions of dollars' worth of livestock every year. They kill many wild animals too. In some areas they kill more deer than hunters do.

* * *

WHO PAYS for all of the animal-related accidents and illnesses? Who pays for the cattle that are killed by dog packs? Who pays the salaries of the people who clean up the thirty-five hundred tons of animal droppings that are left on our streets every day? Who pays for the replacement of the city-owned trees and shrubs that have been killed by millions of gallons of animal urine? Who pays the $500 million that's required to maintain our animal shelters, to pick up our strays, and to dispose of the bodies of the dogs and cats that have been euthanised or struck by cars?

The answer is that, in one way or another, we all do. Even if no one in your family has ever been bitten by a dog, all of you are paying the cost of other people's dog bites through your medical insurance premiums. You may never have been in a car that crashed to avoid hiting an animal, but your family's automobile insurance rates are higher because of the damage that results from such accidents. The taxes on the house in which you live include the cost of cleaning up after the stray animal population of your city. The meat that you eat is more expensive because hundreds of farmers had to replace the cattle that had been ravaged by dogs.

Many people are becoming angry at having to pay for the carelessness of pet owners. In a few large cities where the problem of strays is especially bad, groups of citizens have organized to lobby for laws to ban pets from crowded urban centers. So far, they haven't had much success, but they will continue to be angry as they walk down the streets and see all the animal droppings; as their sleep is disturbed by the night sounds of yowling cats and barking dogs; and as they see the packs of feral dogs that gather in their neighborhoods.

Most of these people don't hate animals. They are saddened when they see a quivering, cringing, half-starved creature rooting about in a sack of garbage. They hear about mass euthanasia and wonder what is happening to the relationship between man and animal.

Many, many years ago, an American Indian tribe told a beautiful tale about the beginnings of that relationship. The tale described a mighty earthquake that rent the earth into two halves. A chasm separated the sections. The animals were left on one side of this chasm, the humans on the other. Most of the beasts seemed unconcerned by the situation. They continued to forage and to care for their young as they always had. The dog, however, was greatly distressed. Whining and whimpering, he spent his time running back and forth along the edge of the crevice.

For a long time, the leader of the humans

watched the unhappy creature. He then turned to the other tribal members. When he had finished speaking to them, they all nodded their heads in agreement. The leader walked to the rim of the chasm, held out his arms, and called, "Come!" The dog looked at him, perked up his ears, and wagged his tail, but didn't jump. Instead, he looked back at the other animals, then down into the bottomless crevice. It was obvious that he was undecided and frightened.

"Come," the man called again, and this time the dog braced his legs and leaped. He barely cleared the great distance. When he arrived on the other side, he clung to the edge of the cliff with his forepaws, while his hind legs tried to gain a foothold in thin air. The men rushed to his aid. With eager hands they pulled him to safety.

From that moment on, according to this ancient legend, man and dog have been inseparable. Through the centuries we took the dog and the cat from their natural states, bred them to our needs and tastes, conditioned them to accept our domain and to be dependent upon us—and now we're abandoning them by the millions.

After thousands of years of domestication, can we really expect these creatures to take care of themselves? "Of course not," say the people who work in animal shelters and humane organizations; the men and women who fill their homes with the strays that appear at their doors; and the officers who patrol the streets in search of starving and injured animals. They know that the solution to the problem of surplus dogs and cats can't wait until next year, or next month, or even next week. It must be started *today*, because today is the time to prevent tomorrow's suffering.

And who's going to have to find that solution? Certainly all of the people who are already involved in animal control and animal rescue can help, but the ultimate responsibility for that solution rests with *all* of us. Every pet owner; everyone who respects the rights of animals; and everyone who's concerned about making our cities a good place to live for both animals and humans will have to work to stop the dog and cat population explosion.

To get right to the bottom line, "the animals will be crying" until you and I care enough to put an end to their suffering.

Index

Abandonment of pets, 56–58, 105–107
American Humane Association (AHA), 21
American Society for the Prevention of Cruelty to Animals (ASPCA), 19–20
Animal control officers. *See* Control officers
The Animals Are Crying (film), 122
Animal shelters. *See* Shelters

Barn cats, 112
Bergh, Henry
  and beginning of humane movement, 17–19
  and ASPCA , 19–21
Breakaway collar, 113

Caging, and emotional problems, 61–62
Carter, Jimmy, 104
Cats
  breeding, 115
  domestication, 13–14
  stewardship of, 111–112
  see also Pets; Strays

Collars, for pets, 113
Control officers
  and catching strays, 49–52
  making the rounds, 86–92
  people problems, 54–58
  tasks of, 52–54
Costs, of animal-related problems, 124–125

Decompression chamber, in killing strays, 62–64
Dog catchers. *See* Control officers
Dogs
  breeding, 114
  domestication, 10–13
  early control methods, 15–16
  stewardship, 110–111
  see also Pets; Strays
Domestication
  of cats, 13–14
  of dogs, 10–13
Dynamo, battered kitten, 40–42

Emergency calls, for animal control, 53–54
Euthanasia, for stray animals, 60–67

Factory farming, 31
Fencing vs. tying, for dogs,
111
Fox, Michael, and pet stewardship, 107–108
Foxtails, as danger for pets,
112–113

Gordon, Barbara, and capture
of iceplant dog, 96–98

Harley, dog that saved owner's
life, 99–101
Humane movement
beginnings, 17–19
early organizations, 19–21
Humane officers. *See* Control
officers
Humane societies, one-person,
70–77
Humane Society of the United
States (HSUS), 26, 29
investigations, 30–31

Iceplant dog (Tucker), capture of, 95–98
Identification (ID) tags for
pets, 113
and finding lost pets, 118,
119, 120
Indian legend, of man and dog,
125–126

Jenson, Tom, and Harley, dog
that saved his life, 99–101
Johnny, dog in "Here's
Boomer" TV series,
101–102

Kullberg, Dr. John, 68

Leash laws, reasons for, 55–56
Leash training
for cats, 111–112
for dogs, 110–111
Lost pets, 116–121

Mahoney, Jean (Dog Lady),
73–75
Morris, cat in TV commer-
cials, 101

Neutering, 113–114

Perry, Hettie (Cat Lady),
70–72
Pet finders, 117–118
Pets
abandonment of, 56–58, 105–
107
collars for, 113
foxtails as danger for, 112–
113
ID tags for, 113
lost, 116–121
stewardship, 107–115
see also Cats; Dogs; Strays
Pet stores, buying animals in,
109
Puppy mills, 109

Rambo, Gib, 60–61, 68
Roadside zoos, 31–32

Sandy, dog in "Annie" show,
102–104

Shelters
  badly run, 23–26
  complaints on, 29–32
  and finding lost pet, 117, 120
  and euthanising of pets, 59–
    61, 65–69
  and irresponsible owners,
    46–48, 68
  tasks of, 3–8
  well run, 26–28
  workers in, 42–48
Smiley, mistreated Beagle, 98–
  99
Sodium pentobarbitol, to
  euthanise animals,
  64–65
Spaying, 113–114
Stewardship, 107–115
Strays
  damage done by, 122–123

street-smart, 50–51
and animal control officers,
  9–10
see also Pets

Training, for dogs, 110
Tucker, iceplant dog, 95–98
Tying vs. fencing, for dogs,
  111

Whitey, stray dog befriended
  by truckers, 94–95
Wright, Phyllis, 68–69, 70, 106
  on inhumane animal shelters,
  26–27

Zoos, roadside, 31–32